Measurement and Evaluation in Music

Measurement and Evaluation in Music

Second Edition

William E. Whybrew
Northern Arizona University

WM. C. BROWN COMPANY PUBLISHERS
Dubuque, Iowa

MUSIC SERIES

Consulting Editor
Frederick W. Westphal
Sacramento State College

Contents

Preface

Since the appearance of the original edition of *Measurement and Evaluation in Music* a resurgence of interest in testing in music has resulted in the publication of several important new measures of musical aptitude and achievement. The current edition includes those significant measures which have appeared since the publication of the first edition of this book.

This text is in large part an outgrowth of the author's experience in teaching graduate courses in measurement and evaluation in music. That experience has revealed a real need for a text suitable for such a course.

Some, of course, would question the need for specialized courses in measurement and evaluation in music in the belief that general courses in educational measurement supply the music teacher, as well as others, with the knowledge in this field which he will find necessary. It is true that general principles of measurement are common to all areas of education, and these the music teacher can learn in the general course. Nearly all such courses, however, ignore aptitude and achievement measures in music, or, at most, do no more than mention that such tests exist and name one or two of the best known.

This lack of attention to specialized fields is quite understandable. It leaves the music teacher ignorant, however, of the measures which are of greatest importance to him. While it might seem a simple matter to apply general principles of test evaluation to measures in specialized fields, experience has shown the author that many students feel the need for a course with specialized emphasis.

Although the testing movement has long been regarded with skepticism by many musicians and teachers, the music profession and the music industry have acknowledged public interest in measurement of aptitude through the presentation of tests of "talent" in quite significant numbers. Not only have several psychologists and teachers interested in this field brought forth such measures, but the number of tests presented by instrument manufacturers and distributors and by various types of institutions in the field of music could comprise a rather extensive bibliography. Needless to say, a wide range of merit is covered by these efforts.

Certainly the music teacher should possess sufficient knowledge of tests and measurements in music to enable him both to select for his own use measures which can best serve his purpose in any given situation and to guide others in similar selections. Experience has shown, unfortunately, that many teachers are not so equipped. Furthermore, those anxious to improve their knowledge of this subject are hindered by lack of a source which will provide them with practical information with particular emphasis upon music.

Some texts in the psychology of music include discussions of existing measures in music. Similar material, usually brief and rather cursory in nature, can be found in various books dealing with principles of music teaching. These sources deal only with existing tests, however, and say little or nothing about general principles and concepts which would enable teachers not only to analyze and evaluate measures which may appear in the future, but also to read critically and intelligently literature pertaining to tests and measurements in their field.

It is the objective of the present work to provide a source from which music teachers and prospective teachers can gain sufficient knowledge, both of testing principles and concepts with special reference to music and of existing measures in the field of music, to enable them to use, to read about intelligently, and to discuss work in this field which has been done in the past and which may be done in the future. It is a further objective to aid music teachers in constructing better informal instruments with which to gauge their students' progress and to evaluate their own teaching.

This book is designed for use by readers in three categories: students in measurement courses such as are included in graduate curricula in music education in many schools; music teachers in the field who wish to inform themselves better about this subject; and undergraduate students in music education courses which make reference to this subject.

No previous knowledge of statistics is required for understanding the material included. Understanding of certain statistical terms and symbols commonly used in test literature obviously is essential to an understanding of testing literature. Such terms and symbols are explained in the text. A separate chapter providing a brief coverage of formulae and procedures used in computing common statistical measures is included for those who wish to make use of it. A number of these measures are extremely useful in course grading. This chapter may be omitted, however, by those who feel no need for it without sacrificing understanding of the essential concepts. It is not the purpose of this text to qualify the reader to devise or construct standardized measures in this field. A more thorough knowledge of testing and test construction in general is essential for such work.

It is the recommendation of the author that the reader gain firsthand knowledge of as many published tests and test batteries as possible. While many have been described in some detail in the text, this material can best serve as a guide to study of the measures themselves.

The author is indebted to many persons for assistance and encouragement in the writing of this book. Specific appreciation must be expressed to Mrs. Truman Lee Kelley, the McGraw-Hill Book Company, W. W. Norton and Company, and the State University of Iowa for permission to use material from publications under their respective control.

CHAPTER 1

Introduction

Needs for Measurement and Evaluation in Music

Measurement is a subject which seems to many to have little in common with music. To some the objectivity and precision implied in measurement are antithetical to the aesthetic nature of music, and not a few musicians have been suspicious of any attempt to associate the two.

Many musicians are called upon frequently, however, to make judgments which result from measurement and evaluation. Anyone who conducts or judges auditions for any purpose is thereby concerned with measurement and evaluation. Teachers in the various areas of music are confronted constantly by the need to appraise the progress of their students for purposes of diagnosis and marking, as are their fellows in other fields. The identification and analysis of students' difficulties is a necessary prerequisite to remedial procedures. Evaluative techniques are of value to the teacher, too, in appraising the effectiveness of his own teaching procedures and materials.

The music teacher's need for sound techniques and procedures in appraisal, therefore, is as great as that of his colleagues in other fields. This is true of both the private studio teacher and the music faculty member, although the more public nature of the latter's position may make his need more apparent. As in other fields, this need is as old as teaching itself.

There probably are few fields other than music in which less attention has been given by teachers and practitioners in general to the development of sound and efficient techniques of measurement and evaluation. Evaluations of musical performance too often have consisted of generalized impressions, formed in a rather haphazard manner and subject to pressures and feelings of the moment. While the nature of music and much music instruction is such as to make an objective approach difficult, many examiners and auditioners probably are guilty of insufficient effort toward this end.

There are few fields, too, in which good guidance is more vital. The great waste of talent, and of money and effort by the untalented, has been of concern to music educators for many years. Psychologists and educators have been prompted by this concern to seek out measures which might help to reduce or to prevent such waste. The result has been the construction of a number of tests which attempt to provide information important to good guidance in music.

At the same time that there is a need for improved methods of measurement and evaluation in music, there is another, less positive but no less important, need among musicians and music teachers for knowledge of principles of measurement and evaluation. The need for tools for guidance which has spurred on psychologists and educators in their attempts to devise sound measures has produced a number of "talent tests" of highly questionable basis and authorship. It is doubtful that there is any area of education in which charlatanism and quackery have been as prevalent in measurement and evaluation as in music. Music teachers, especially those in public institutions, must be capable of separating the sound from the spurious and of guiding their students and their students' parents accordingly. The careful scrutiny and investigation of musical aptitude tests, guided by familiarity with legitimate principles and procedures in measurement, will expose those of doubtful foundation.

Measures of musical aptitude and achievement also are essential tools in some research studies. Increased interest in research in music education, especially in musical learning and methods of teaching, has expanded the need for valid measures of musical aptitude and achievement and for knowledge of such measures. Those who utilize tests for research purposes must select tests with equal care. Results of a study which depends upon a measure of aptitude or achievement can be no better than the tool it uses.

The Historical Background of Testing

Attempts at quantitative measurement of various human traits and abilities developed during the latter half of the nineteenth century. Increased concern for the welfare and care of the mentally retarded had led to the establishment of many special institutions for the care of these unfortunates, and with the growth of such institutions came a need for some uniform method of identifying and classifying such cases.

The early work of physicians and physiologists in classifying and in working with the mentally retarded gave impetus to the development of a school of experimental psychology. The first laboratory for experimental psychology was established at Leipzig, Germany, in 1879 by Wilhelm Wundt. Wundt and his associates were concerned primarily with analysis of consciousness and the identification of uniformities or generalizations of behavior. Wundt exhibited little interest in differences between individuals, but he had a strong influence upon later psychologists whose work led in this direction.

At first the psychologists were mainly interested in the same type of measurements which had concerned the physiologists. These were measures of sensitivity to visual, auditory, and other sensory stimuli, and of simple reaction time. Gradually, however, their attention turned to other matters such as measurement of the rate of learning, of the perceptual span, of the timing of various types of mental tasks, matters perhaps more aptly characterized as psychological.

These early psychological experiments made apparent the need for rigorous control of conditions under which they were made. It was found that various factors, such as wording of directions, could significantly influence the results attained by the subject. It thus became obvious that experiments with all subjects should be conducted under standardized conditions. Such standardization of procedure is now viewed as an important factor in psychological testing.

An English biologist, Sir Francis Galton, was a prominent figure in the development of testing. Galton was deeply interested in heredity, and he conducted extensive investigations into degrees of resemblance between related individuals. In order to determine the degree of resemblance between such persons it was necessary to find some method of measuring their characteristics. Galton devised a number of tests and measuring instruments which are still known either in their original form or in modified forms. Best known among these, perhaps, are the Galton bar for visual discrimination of length, the Galton whistle for determining the highest audible pitch, and graduated series of weights for measuring kinaesthetic discrimination. It was Galton's belief that tests of sensory discrimination could give significant indication of a person's intellect. Galton made a significant contribution to the testing movement, also, through his application of statistical methods to the analysis of test data.

James McKeen Cattell was an American psychologist whose work was influenced by both Wundt and Galton. After obtaining his doctorate at Leipzig, he came into contact with Galton while lecturing at Cambridge University. His own interest in the measurement of individual differences was stimulated by this latter contact, and upon his return to the United States he took an active part in the establishment of laboratories for experimental psychology and in the development of the testing movement.

Cattell shared Galton's view that tests of sensory discrimination and simple reaction time could be used to measure the intellect. He devised a series of tests of simple sensory and motor performances which were administered annually to numbers of college students in an effort to determine the relationship between such measures and academic attainments. Unfortunately, the revelation that these tests showed little relationship with college work had an adverse effect upon testing in the United States which was felt until the publication of Alfred Binet's work in 1905. Nonetheless, Cattell exerted a strong influence on the development of testing through his students and his journals.

E. L. Thorndike, a student of Cattell just before the end of the nineteenth century, was another influential figure in the development of standardized educational tests. Active as a teacher and in research, Thorndike had a broad influence in the spread of objective measurement in education.

The work of Binet, resulting in the Binet-Simon Scale and its subsequent revisions, has made his probably the best known name in the field of intelligence testing. The first Binet-Simon Scale, which appeared in 1905, was intended as a preliminary and tentative instrument and was succeeded in 1908 by a revised version. Although sensory tests were included, these scales used a higher proportion of verbal content than most test series of that time. Further revisions of the Binet scales were made in later years. That best known in the United States was the so-called Stanford-Binet, developed at Stanford University under the direction of L. M. Terman. This test was the first to use the concept of the Intelligence Quotient (I.Q.), the ratio between mental age and chronological age.

The Binet scale and its various revisions were individual tests, i.e., they could be administered to only one person at a time. With the entrance of the United States into World War I in 1917, psychologists recognized the need for methods of quickly classifying the huge masses of men absorbed by the army. The work of psychologists in answer to this pressing need resulted in the construction of intelligence tests which could be administered to large groups.

The release of the army tests for civilian use after the war gave tremendous impetus to the testing movement. Group intelligence tests were devised for persons of all ages and all types. Standardized tests for most school skills and for the content areas of the school program were developed, and testing programs were instituted in many school systems. Various types of achievement tests, personality questionnaires, and personality inventories came into being. Simplified instruction and administration procedures possible with the group tests were an important factor in this testing boom.

The nineteen twenties represent the period of greatest growth of the testing movement. Not only did the production of tests multiply, but tests were administered widely and, unfortunately, somewhat indiscriminately. Test results were often accepted uncritically and unwisely applied. In their enthusiasm, some persons lost sight of the fact that tests were still crude instruments and that care must be exercised in their use and in the interpretation of results.

When test results failed to fulfill the extravagant promises made for them by their overly-enthusiastic proponents, critics leaped to the attack. Specific tests and the philosophy of testing in general both were subjected to criticisms. These strictures sometimes were just, but as often they were as extravagant as were the praises of the enthusiastic proponents. By provoking the skepticism and hostility toward testing which resulted from the failure of the tests to meet unreasonable expectations, the overly-enthusiastic proponents of objective measurement may have done as much to retard as to advance the progress of the testing movement.

The second decade of the twentieth century witnessed an increased interest in the measurement of specific aptitudes. During this period psychologists and educators turned their efforts toward attempts to measure the potential of an individual for accomplishment in specific fields of endeavor.

One of the earliest and best known attempts to measure specific aptitude came in the field of music with the appearance in 1919 of Carl E. Seashore's *Measures of Musical Talent.*

The nature of musical talent had attracted the interest of psychologists during the nineteenth century. Several studies, dating from shortly before the turn of the century, were published listing traits which the authors considered to be important elements in musical talent. Several of the lists resulted from analysis of the abilities and personalities of persons known to be gifted musically.

The lists showed a variance of opinion both as to the number of traits and abilities important to musicality and to the relative importance of these various factors. These variances undoubtedly were due to the types of investigations made as well as to the highly complex nature of musical talent itself. Among the elements appearing most consistently in the different reports are various types of sensory capacity, particularly those related to pitch sensitivity. A number of reports also placed some emphasis upon retentive capacity.

The battery of tests which Seashore devised consisted of six measures, one each of pitch discrimination, intensity or loudness discrimination, discrimination of time intervals, perception of differences between rhythmic patterns, discrimination of degrees of consonance, and retention of tonal patterns. In his writings Seashore emphasized that these capacities by no means represented the total complex of musical talent, but were important *measurable* elements among what he termed "a hierarchy of talents."[1] These measures were widely used and subjected to considerable experimentation in order to detect weaknesses and to improve procedures. As a result of wide experience with the original Seashore battery, a revised version was issued in 1939 by Seashore, Lewis, and Saetveit. Several important changes were made in this revised battery, which will be described in detail in Chapter 8.

The original Seashore measures were followed in 1930 by the publication of a battery of tests devised by Jacob Kwalwasser and Peter Dykema. This battery covered much the same area as the Seashore, and in addition it attempted to measure some aspects of imagery and aesthetic sensitivity in music. In 1934 the Drake Musical Memory Test appeared.

No more measures of musical aptitude were published until the appearance of the revision of the Seashore measures in 1939. These were followed by a set of tests by Lowell Mason Tilson, which was copyrighted in 1941 by the Fred Gretsch Manufacturing Company. These, too, seemed to be based on psychological beliefs similar to those of Seashore.

During the next two decades tests and test batteries dealing with musical aptitude were published by Herbert Wing, Kwalwasser, E. Thayer Gaston, Raleigh Drake, and the team of Harvey Whistler and Louis Thorpe. Several of these revealed a shift in psychological theory of the measurement of musical aptitude,

---

[1]C. E. Seashore, *Psychology of Musical Talent.* New York: Silver, Burdett and Company, 1919. p. 6.

giving less importance to sensory capacities and greater emphasis to perceptual responses. More recent measures of musical aptitude have been published by Edwin Gordon and Arnold Bentley.

In addition to these measures of musical aptitude, which have been made available in published form, a number of others were devised and described in journals and monographs during the four decades which followed the appearance of the original Seashore measures. Among these were group measures by Schoen, Ortmann, Madison, and Lundin. Still others constructed or suggested tests and test batteries suitable for individual administration.

Measures of musical aptitude shared in the general enthusiasm which greeted the testing movement during the nineteen twenties. Many music educators welcomed the appearance of these objective measures, seeing in them an answer to some of the thorniest problems with which they were confronted in their work. Now it would be possible to identify at a relatively early age those who possessed the potential for accomplishment in music, thus enabling the teacher both to encourage the talented and, perhaps more important, to prevent the frustration of the eager but untalented. Knowledge of a student's potential, obtained through objective measurement, would enable the teacher to set up realistic goals for the student and to aid him more wisely in attaining those goals.

As in other fields, the enthusiasm of some exceeded the bounds of reason. Claims and predictions were made regarding testing and other forms of objective measurement in music which turned the skepticism of many musicians into open antagonism. Many music educators, finding that tests did not provide all of the answers for which they had hoped, joined the ranks of the critics. The first wave of enthusiastic approval subsided before the onrush of mounting criticism.

Perhaps because he was the pioneer, perhaps because he appeared to be the most explicit in statement of his beliefs, Seashore and his *Measures of Musical Talent* bore the brunt of the attacks. Since these measures were subjected to wider and more intensive study and were used in more related investigations than any other tests in the field, they became the subject of many articles and statements, both in approbation and condemnation.

Controversy about musical aptitude and its measurement has continued to rage. Test authors and other psychologists and educators have debated theories concerning the estimation of musical potential, while many teachers have continued to question the value of such measures in general. That interest in finding adequate measures is still very much alive, however, is evidenced by the continued appearances of new tests during the last 15 years.

Measurement of achievement in music by standardized tests seems to have attracted less interest generally than has the measurement of aptitude. It has, at least, excited far less controversy. Nonetheless, the number of measures of various kinds of achievement in music which have appeared in a fairly steady stream during the past five decades attests to the interest of many music educators.

The first measure of musical achievement to appear was the *Beach Music Test*, by Beach and Schrammel, which was first published in 1920. A revised edition appeared in 1930 and a reprinting in 1938. Since then measures have appeared periodically except during the decade of the nineteen forties, which seems to have produced no tests of this type. While many of these tests of achievement deal principally with knowledge of symbols of notation and other rudiments of music theory, several delve into more active aspects of performance such as sight singing and actual instrumental proficiency.

The measurement of musical taste and of music appreciation are other areas which have attracted the interest of researchers in musical measurement. Measures of taste have been included in some musical aptitude test batteries, and many research studies have used measures devised by the investigators. The lack of absolute standards of musical taste and even of a universally accepted definition of music appreciation, however, makes objective measurement in these areas extremely difficult—a fact perhaps made evident by the dearth of published measures.

Uses of Musical Aptitude Measures

Authors of early measures of aptitude for musical accomplishment emphasized the value of their work for the guidance of students, and it may safely be assumed that such a purpose was a prime objective of these psychologists and educators. If a child's potential for musical accomplishment could be assessed before beginning musical training, they suggested, frustration and waste could be avoided. The eager but inept could be advised to direct their energies toward endeavors for which their talents seemed better suited, while those unaware of their own potential for achievement in music could be shown a possible avenue for satisfying and rewarding endeavor.

Musical aptitude measures have been used for such guidance in varying ways. In some school systems such tests are administered on a so-called "dragnet" basis, in which every child at a certain grade level is given the test. The resulting scores then are used in encouraging or discouraging musical endeavor. Such a practice, used in the Rochester, New York, public schools, was cited in support of musical aptitude tests a number of years ago. It was the stated belief of the supervisor of music in that city that use of the Seashore *Measures of Musical Talent* had a significant influence in reducing the drop-out rate in the instrumental program.[2] Others have found similar values in musical aptitude tests.

In some other schools, although they are not administered on the "dragnet" basis, aptitude measures are used as a criterion for selection among students. The selection may be among those students applying for school-owned instruments, for instrumental instruction, for admission to a select vocal or instrumental ensemble, or for some similar purpose. Various types of musical achievement tests are also used in some schools to screen applicants for select musical organizations.

Standardized measures of musical aptitude have also been used extensively in certain types of psychological and genetic studies. Investigation of relationship between musicality and other traits, of differences between races and sexes, etc., obviously can be facilitated by a valid measure of aptitude for music.

---

[2]Peter W. Dykema and Karl W. Gehrkens, *High School Music*. Boston: C. C. Birchard and Company, 1941. p. 589. For a more recent evaluation of the use of the Seashore measures for guidance in the Rochester schools, see Ruth C. Larson, "Finding and Guiding Musical Talent," *Mus. Ed. J.*, 42:1, 1955, pp. 22-25.

It is unfortunate that, in many instances in which aptitude measures have been used for selection, too great weight has been given to the results attained on the test. This has led to the belief on the part of many teachers that aptitude measures have been proposed as the principal, if not the sole, criterion for selection. Many, finding them inadequate for such a role, have thereupon summarily dismissed the measures as a waste of time. Some teachers, of course, are opposed to any attempt at selection of students for musical training, holding that opportunity should be given to all who wish to try.

Circumstances often may dictate some type of selection, however, regardless of the philosophy of the teacher or administrator. Suppose a situation, far from imaginary, in which applicants for school-owned instruments exceed the number of instruments available. Obviously, some selection must be made. In such a case it does not seem good sense to encourage those students who seem least likely to benefit from the opportunity for specialized instruction in music. Even in such a case, however, an aptitude test cannot by itself solve the problem, but a valid measure can supply the teacher with more information about the students concerned. The teacher then must weigh all the factors to be considered in reaching his decision.

It is as sources of information that measures of musical aptitude and of musical achievement should be regarded. A valid measure of musical aptitude can provide the teacher with specific knowledge of students' potentialities, thus enabling him to know his students better. In certain situations an objective measure can be of great help in diagnosing a student's difficulties and, consequently, in helping him to overcome them. Is a student's failure to match pitches or to sing in tune due to poor discrimination or to some other factor such as poor vocal control? What can be expected of student A, who experiences difficulty in following short passages of music accompanied by explanation? Is a deficient sense of pitch or inability to retain tonal patterns for a brief period responsible for his difficulty, or is lack of attention and effort the cause of his unsatisfactory progress? Valid objective measures of pitch discrimination and tonal memory can supply information which will help in finding solutions to these and similar problems.

It is as tools for guidance and teaching that aptitude measures can be of greatest value. Even in such a function, however, tests have definite limitations. Musical aptitude measures can at best supply only limited information about the students to whom they are administered. Many other factors such as interest, general aptitude for learning, motor control, and pertinacity must be considered in conjunction with aptitude rankings, and guidance must be based upon the total picture. It would seem, however, that any measure which contributes to the teacher's knowledge of his students is a significant tool for use in his work. The sincere teacher will be eager to know as much as possible about those whom he must guide.

SUMMARY

Attempts to measure various human traits and abilities began in the latter half of the nineteenth century, stimulated by the establishment and growth of institutions for the mentally retarded. The measurement movement spread from Europe to the United States largely through the work of Americans who experienced this work in the European centers of experimental psychology.

The need for classifying huge masses of men during World War I gave rise to the group test, and the release of army tests for civilian use stimulated a boom in objective measurement in the period following the end of the war. The first standardized measures of musical aptitude were devised by Carl E. Seashore early in this period.

Measures of musical aptitude have shared the enthusiastic acceptance and subsequent suspicion and even denunciation accorded objective measures in general during the past four decades. Their true worth undoubtedly lies between the extravagant claims of early enthusiasts and the bitter criticisms of later skeptics.

While measurement of musical achievement has excited far less controversy than has the measurement of aptitude, the appearance of a number of measures of various types of musical accomplishment indicates a continued interest in standardized tests in this area. These tests have been concerned with some aspects of performance as well as knowledge of music rudiments.

Measures of musical aptitude have been used in various situations for selection of talented students and in certain kinds of psychological and genetic studies. They should be looked upon as sources of certain types of information only, and when used for guidance should be used intelligently and discreetly in combination with other sources of information.

QUESTIONS FOR DISCUSSION

1. What needs has the music teacher for knowledge of principles and procedures in measurement and evaluation?
2. From your own experience as student and teacher, what seem to be the prevalent practices in evaluating musical performance?
3. What need, which later had to be satisfied in psychological testing, was revealed by early psychological experiments?
4. How can valid measures of musical aptitude aid the school music teacher?
5. What place have measures of musical aptitude had in the development of testing?
6. Why may standardized measures of musical achievement have attracted less attention than similar measures of aptitude?
7. In what ways have measures of musical aptitude been used?
8. How can measures of musical aptitude be used in the school music program? What precautions should be observed?

RECOMMENDED READINGS

Anastasi, Anne. *Psychological Testing.* 3rd ed., New York: Macmillan, 1968. Chapter 1.

Seashore, C. E. *Psychology of Music.* New York: McGraw-Hill Book Co., 1938. Chapter 24.

Stanley, Julian C. *Measurement in Today's Schools.* 4th ed., New York: Prentice-Hall, 1964. Chapter 2.

CHAPTER 2

Interpretation of
Test Literature

In order to interpret literature dealing with testing, an understanding of certain common terminology is essential. Certain statistical devices and terms are referred to in test manuals in giving information necessary for the understanding and evaluation of the test. Research reports and other studies useful to the teacher in evaluating tests and their uses also must make use of these common basic terms.

Since some readers may be interested only in sufficient understanding of these terms to permit intelligent interpretation of test literature, the present chapter will be directed toward this end. Some will feel, however, that the surest road to understanding of the meaning of these terms and of the statistical measures to which they refer probably lies through actual computation of the measures. Some may be interested in the computations of some of the measures, too, because they are very useful in course grading. These persons will find formulae and procedures for such computations in Chapter 3.

Before explaining terms which pertain to tests themselves, it seems prudent to define a few terms which are applied to the persons involved in a test situation. The reader frequently will encounter the term *test subject* or, perhaps, just *subject* with *test* implied. *Test subjects* are persons to whom a test is administered, i.e., persons who take a test. This term usually is not used to refer to the subject matter, or content, of a test.

The term *population* as used in test literature may be somewhat confusing to some, although it really retains its literal meaning. In this context it refers to all those persons who have in common certain traits or characteristics. We thus may refer to the population of fifth grade pupils, meaning all pupils in all fifth grades. Or we may refer to a more limited population, such as fifth grade students in one particular state or in a certain city. In any case, the *population* includes *all* persons in that particular category, all persons who may be identified by the criteria used to describe the category.

A population is distinguished from a *sample*. The latter is a segment of a population, a segment chosen to represent a population. Since it usually is impossible or impracticable to administer a test to an entire population for purposes of standardization (see following), it is the usual practice to use samples of the population to which the test is to apply.

Standardized Tests

Certain tests are referred to as *standardized tests*. A standardized test is one which has been so devised that it can be administered to different groups of subjects at different times in widely separated places in such a way that the results can be compared. This means that not only must the test content be fixed, but also that the method and details of administration be carefully worked out and described so that the test can be given in the identical way upon different occasions. It means, further, that scoring procedures must be given the same careful attention so that test papers can be scored by different persons without the occurrence of discrepancies which would invalidate the comparison of results from different testings. Standardized tests, then, may be defined as those tests which have been so devised and set up that they can be administered and scored in a uniform way upon different occasions by different persons. Standardized tests are distinguished from more informal tests which are devised for use in a specific, limited situation in which the test author is available to interpret and administer the test, to score the answers, and to interpret the results.

An obvious requisite of a standardized test is objectivity. Only when any kind of subjective evaluation of answers is completely avoided can scoring procedures be properly standardized. Objectivity itself, however, is not synonymous with standardization.

Standardization of a measure is a lengthy and involved process. While informal teacher-made tests should possess many of the same qualities which we hope to find in the standardized test, e.g., validity and reliability, standardization necessitates more thorough and more extensive procedures in the preparation of the test. After the test content has been carefully chosen, the test must be "tried out" on carefully selected samples of the population or populations for which the test is intended. If a test of musical achievement is intended for use with junior high school students, for example, it must be administered to sample groups of students at this level. It is of extreme importance that such samples be chosen with care. It is absolutely essential that they be truly representative of the population with which the test is to be used if the test is to be truly standardized. If the sample is not truly representative, any comparisons made with the established norms may be quite invalid. An adequate description of the samplings used and of the standardization procedure in general should be made readily available to users of the test so that invalid comparisons will not be made.

Norms

Norms are scores which have been empirically established as typical for a population, i.e., typical for all persons grouped according to common characteristics or criteria. Thus, norms might be established for various purposes for seventh graders, for college freshmen, for high school band members, or for any other category of persons. The derivation of such scores usually is an important part of the standardization procedure, and most standardized tests are provided with such tables. Although other aspects of a test may be standardized without providing norms, an important value of standardization—comparison of subjects' scores with those of larger populations—is lost without them.

It should be pointed out that norms represent *typical*, or normal, performance on a test. They should not be viewed as standards or goals to be attained. If a group of subjects attains the norm on a test, this means that they are average, that they measure up to the sample or typical group. Whether or not this might represent desirable attainment for this particular group would depend upon other factors and could be determined only through further study.

In using a table of norms for comparison of scores it is important that the appropriate table be used. A set of scores may represent normal performance on a test for fifth graders, for college freshmen, for male adolescents, for college music majors, or for the general population; in short, for any type of group. A score representing a certain level of achievement in one group, e.g., fifth graders, may represent a quite different level of achievement in a different type of group, e.g., sixth graders. On the *Drake Musical Memory Test*, for example, a boy in the 11 to 13 year age group who made 72 mistakes would do as well as approximately 49 per cent of the sample group of that age used in standardizing the test. A like score for a boy in the 13 to 15 year age bracket, however, would be up to only about 32 per cent of the sample group in that age bracket.[1] Comparison with an inappropriate table, obviously, would be very misleading.

Percentiles, Deciles, Quartiles

Norms are presented in various ways, according to the type of test concerned and the age or grade level at which it is to be used.

The actual score attained, or the number of points accumulated, by a subject on a given test is known as a *raw score*. This

---

[1] Raleigh M. Drake, *Manual of Directions for Musical Memory Test.* Bloomington, Illinois: Public School Publishing Co., 1934. p. 11.

score by itself tells little concerning the subject's achievement or standing on the test. To say that John Smith scored 89 on a particular test is meaningless. If the maximum number of points attainable also is made known, the score has a little more meaning, but still it tells little about John's standing. Let us suppose that the maximum attainable score on this test, on which John scored 89 points, was 110. Now we know that John scored 89 points out of a possible 110. But what does this tell us about John's achievement, particularly in relation to that of others? If John were one of a group of 50 who took the test, the significance of his score of 89 is quite different if 45 of the group scored above 89 than if 45 of the group scored below 89.

In order to enable the interpreter of test results to ascertain the standing of a particular score in a group, or to compare scores attained by certain test subjects with those attained by typical groups, norms frequently are couched in terms of ranks.

A *percentile rank* (also known as *centile rank*) shows the standing of a raw score in a group divided into one hundred levels. If a raw score of 90 on a test is found to stand in the 70th percentile rank, for example, this means that 70 per cent of the scores in that group are below 90.

A table of percentile norms shows the standings, in terms of one hundred levels, of the raw scores attained on the test by the standardization subjects. If the standardization procedure has been careful and sound, the standardization subjects have been chosen so as to reflect accurately the type of population described, e.g., fifth and sixth grade students, or non-selected college freshmen, or college students majoring in music, etc. A percentile rank, then, shows the standing of a raw score, and of persons attaining that score, in relation to the scores of the trial group. Thus, if a college freshman music major attains a raw score of 75 on a standardized musical achievement test, and it is found that in the accompanying table of norms for that type of individual (i.e., college freshman music major) a raw score of 75 stands in the 53rd percentile rank, it may be assumed that 53 per cent of all college freshman music majors would stand below this individual. While there are some dangers in a simplified assumption such as this, it is about as accurate as is usually possible, and in most cases will not prove too misleading for practical purposes.

Percentiles and percentile ranks should not be confused with a per cent score or grade on a test. The latter is a percentage of the total number of points attainable on the test and actually tells nothing about an individual's standing in a group or on a standardized test. The widespread conditioning of the public to per cent scores and grades not infrequently has led to unfortunate misinterpretations of test scores by unqualified individuals.

Some tables of norms use *decile* ranks instead of percentiles. Similar in principle to percentiles, deciles represent the standings of raw scores when a distribution is divided into ten levels rather than into one hundred. It is, obviously, a less precise indication of relative standing.

Distributions sometimes are marked off into *quartiles*. It probably is already apparent to the reader that quartiles divide the group of scores numerically into four equal segments. The first quartile is the point below which 25 per cent of the scores fall. The second quartile is that point below which 50 per cent of the scores fall, and the third quartile marks off the lower 75 per cent from the top quarter. The first quartile is abbreviated Q_1, and the third is indicated by Q_3. While the second quartile logically might be represented by Q_2, this symbol is rarely used. The second quartile always is the same as the median (see following) and usually is expressed as the latter.

Percentiles, deciles, and quartiles (as distinguished from percentile ranks, decile ranks, and quartile ranks) actually are *points* along a distribution which separate the ranks. The terms frequently are used somewhat loosely, however, and this distinction is not consistently observed. The respective ranks are of more importance in relation to tables of norms, and it is the ranks which are referred to most frequently in test manuals and in other literature pertaining to tests even when the word rank is omitted. The context of the material usually will make clear to the reader which meaning is intended.

Ranks usually are numbered from the lowest to the highest, i.e., rank one contains the lowest scores. There are exceptions to this practice, however. Such a deviation generally is quite apparent from a perusal of the table, and it should cause the reader no trouble if reasonable care is exercised in examining the data. Rank is more meaningful than a raw score. At a glance one can tell from the percentile rank or the decile rank how any subject compares on a test with others like him, assuming that the test has been administered under comparable conditions.

Raw scores are also converted frequently into *standard scores.* Since understanding of the latter requires knowledge of the standard deviation, discussion of standard scores is reserved for a later portion of this chapter.

Obviously, the degree of care which has been exerted in establishing norms for a test is of utmost importance. The number of cases used, and the degree of accuracy with which they represent the total population of the type described, are highly significant factors. Other things being equal, the greater the number of cases used in establishing norms, the more likely are the latter to represent "normal" performance for that type of population. If cases not typical of the population described are included in establishing norms, of course, the validity of the norms is seriously impaired. For example, if, in ascertaining "normal" performance for college liberal arts majors on a measure of musical achievement or musical knowledge, a number of scores attained by music majors are included, the resulting norms probably will not fairly represent performance to be expected of liberal arts students.

Measures of Central Tendency

Very often comparison of performances of groups on a particular test is desirable for various reasons. The desired comparisons may be between classes in the same school, between classes in different schools, between a particular class or group and a standardization sample, or between other selected groups. In such cases a measure of central tendency, which helps to describe group performance, is a valuable aid.

Measures of central tendency, also known as averages in measurement terminology, help to show how a group of scores tend to distribute themselves within the range of scores, and particularly how they tend to group or cluster around certain scores. Three such measures are commonly used for various purposes. These are the *mean,* the *median,* and the *mode.*

Perhaps the most frequently used measure of central tendency is the mean. Its use in many phases of everyday life is so common that to a great many people "the average" is that which more accurately is called the *mean*. Simply stated the mean is calculated by adding the scores in a group and dividing the sum by the number of scores. Thus, the mean of the five scores 10, 12, 15, 18, and 25 is 16 $\left(\dfrac{10+12+15+18+25}{5} = 16\right)$.

When a relatively small number of scores is involved, this direct method of computing the mean is quite practicable. When the number of scores renders this "long" method impracticable, however, or when the scores are grouped, the mean can be calculated by formula. For this formula the reader is referred to Chapter 3.

The mean frequently is abbreviated M.

Another measure of central tendency used nearly as frequently as the mean, but usually for somewhat different purposes, is the *median*. This is the midpoint, in numbers, of a group of scores; that point above which lie half of the scores in a distribution and below which lie the other half. The median is the same as the 50th percentile and the second quartile in any distribution.

The *mid-score* often is used interchangeably with the median, although a distinction between them actually exists. The mid-score actually is a score in the distribution when the latter contains an odd number of scores. Thus, in the foregoing small sample distribution given, 15 would be the mid-score. To consider it also the median would do no harm in this case as in any odd-number distribution. In a distribution containing an even number of scores, however, the median does not correspond to any score in the group. It then is found by interpolating between the two halves of the distribution. Thus, if a score of 17 were added to the group of scores in the example (resulting in a distribution of 10, 12, 15, 17, 18, 25) the median would be 16, falling midway between the upper three scores and the lower three.

The median is found by counting the scores. With grouped distributions, a method which is described in Chapter 3 can be used. The median frequently is abbreviated Mdn.

One other measure of central tendency may be encountered in test literature, although it is not used as frequently as the mean or the median. This is the *mode.* It is the score of greatest frequency in a distribution, the score attained by the greatest number of cases. It is possible to have two or even more modes in a distribution. If two scores in a distribution are attained by an equal number of subjects, a number greater than that attaining any other score, that distribution is called *bi-modal.*

Which measure of central tendency is the best to use depends upon the purpose for which it is to be used. The mean is influenced by a few extreme scores at either end of the scale and, therefore, it is not the best measure to employ when such influence is to be avoided. In such cases the median is to be preferred. When it is desirable to take into account such extreme scores, however, the mean obviously is preferable to the median. In general, the mean is the most stable measure of central tendency. It is safe to say that the mode is least frequently the best measure of central tendency to use.

Measures of Variability

A further aid in describing a distribution is a measure of variability. Such a measure shows how a group of scores tends to scatter or spread throughout the distribution. In this way, the measure of variability supplements the measure of central tendency.

A simple illustration will make clear the need for such a supplement in describing a distribution. Take the five scores 30, 40, 50, 60, 70 and the series 10, 30, 50, 70, 90. If these two sets of scores were described by a measure of central tendency alone, they would appear to be identical. In each case both the mean and the median, or more properly the mid-score, are 50. The two series, however, actually are far from identical. This would be revealed by a measure of variability.

The simplest measure of variability is the *range.* This consists of the arithmetic difference between the highest and the lowest scores in a distribution. The range, obviously, is a rather crude indication of the spread of scores in a distribution, since it can be unduly influenced by one exceptional score at either end of the scale. Let us suppose, for example, that in a distribution containing 20 scores 19 of those scores fall between 60 and 80, but that one score, for whatever reason, is only 25. The range would tell us only that the 20 scores lie between 25 and 80, thus giving a very inaccurate description of the general spread of these scores. Since it is such a relatively crude measure, the range is not frequently used to describe the variability of a distribution.

The most frequently used measure of variability is the *standard deviation*, abbreviated SD, S, or σ (sigma)[2]. The standard deviation is computed from the mean score and is based upon the deviations of the several scores from the mean. Between the scores lying at one unit of standard deviation above and below the mean, respectively, fall 68.26 per cent of the scores in any normal distribution. Between the scores lying two units of standard deviation above and below the mean fall 95.4 per cent of the cases in the distribution, and three units of sigma on each side of the mean will include 99.8 per cent of the cases in the distribution. Thus, if in a particular distribution of scores the mean score is 90 and the standard deviation is found to be 10, 68.26 per cent of the scores in that group will be between 80 and 100, 95.4 per cent of the scores will be between 70 and 110, and 99.8 per cent between 60 and 120. The standard deviation, therefore, gives the observer very quickly a good idea of how widely the scores on a test scattered among the group. It is a good indication of the general degree of homogeneity of the group, and, as we shall see in Chapter 4, this is an important factor in interpreting the reliability coefficient of a test.

When the median is used to show the central tendency of a group of scores, variability usually is expressed by another statistical measure, the *quartile deviation*. This is also known as the *semi-interquartile range* and it is abbreviated Q. The *interquartile* range is the score distance between the first and third quartiles or, to use synonymous terms, the 25th and 75th percentiles. It includes, therefore, 50 per cent of the scores in a distribution. The semi-interquartile range, or quartile deviation, is half the interquartile range and tells how far, on the average, the quartile points lie

---

[2]In some literature S or SD is used to designate the standard deviation of a sample, σ to designate the standard deviation of a population.

from the median. For example, if, in a given distribution, a raw score of 97 is found to lie at the 25th percentile and a raw score of 200 at the 75th percentile, the interquartile range is equal to 200 - 97, or 103. We would also know that 50 per cent of the scores in the distribution lie between 97 and 200. Q, the quartile deviation, is then equal to $\frac{200 - 97}{2}$, or 51.5.

Still another measure of variability, the *mean deviation*, consists of the arithmetic mean of the deviations of the separate scores in a distribution from the central tendency, usually the mean. It is calculated by obtaining the sum of the deviations of the several scores from the mean score, or possibly the median or the mode, and dividing this sum by the number of scores in the distribution. The mean deviation, which is abbreviated MD, is also known as the *average deviation* (AD) and the *mean variation* (MV). It is seldom used in modern literature, but it may be encountered in older material.

Which measure of variability is to be preferred again depends upon the purpose for which the measure is to be used. The standard deviation, like the mean from which it is computed, is significantly influenced by extreme scores. The quartile deviation, on the other hand, is not and so is a better choice when such influence is to be avoided. The standard deviation is the most stable measure of variability, and is the most frequently used in test literature. It seems safe to say that the range is, in general, the poorest measure of variability for most purposes.

Measures of Relationship

Another basic statistical concept which has great importance in literature concerning testing is the *coefficient of correlation*. This is the most frequently used, and hence most important, expression of relationship between two entities. It can be used to show the relationship between two sets of scores, between ratings, between test scores and ratings, between any two kinds of measurements, etc. Since the common methods of investigating the validity and the reliability of tests make use of such relationships, these characteristics are very frequently expressed by means of a coefficient of correlation, which then is called a *validity co-efficient* or a *reliability coefficient*. (See Chapter 4).

A coefficient of correlation is expressed as a decimal, and it may have a value ranging from $+1.00$ to -1.00. If the person at the top of one group of scores or ratings also stands at the top of the correlated group, and the same person stands second in both groups, and so on through the two groups of scores, the correlation is said to be perfect positive, and the coefficient is $+1.00$. If the order is exactly reversed, with the person standing at the head of one group ranked last in the other, etc., the correlation is perfect negative and the coefficient would be -1.00. A coefficient of 0.00 expresses complete lack of relationship. Perfect correlations of either positive or negative character are extremely rare.

Two methods of determining correlation are in general use. The simpler of the two is based upon the differences in the rank orders of the two sets of scores or series of measures. The best procedure for determining this kind of correlation is known as the Spearman rho (ρ) method. It is practicable only when small numbers of scores are involved.

A more exact measure of relationship is provided by the product-moment method, resulting in the so-called Pearson r. This method is based upon the deviations from their respective means of the scores in the two sets or series involved. This method is used more frequently than the Spearman rank-difference procedure.

The interpretation of correlation coefficients is a very important, yet far from simple, affair. A number of factors must be considered in evaluating any coefficient of correlation. Important among them is the nature of the variables concerned, since a higher degree of correlation is found customarily between certain variables than between others. It has been usual, for example, to find considerably higher correlations between general intelligence test scores and school grades than between vocational aptitude test scores and vocational success. As a consequence an r of .50 might be judged quite significant for the latter area, whereas it would be considered rather low for the former.

The range of variability and the size of each of the variables being correlated also have a significant effect upon the coefficient of correlation. If test scores or ratings are involved, then the reliabilities of these scores or ratings must be considered in evalua-ting the correlation coefficient. The purpose for which the test is to be used also is important if a test is one of the variables correlated. If the test is to be used to rank individuals within a group it should produce a higher coefficient when correlated with some other variable than it need if its purpose is to distinguish between those who seem likely and those who seem unlikely to succeed.

Verbal descriptions for correlation coefficients are rather hazard-ous undertakings due to the number of factors which must influence the interpretation of any coefficient. A number of writers, however, have given very general verbal descriptions to aid the student. These differ slightly from one another, but in general they can be summed up as follows:

from .00 to ± .15 or .20 indifferent or negligible relationship

from ± .15 or .20 to ± .35 or .40 low correlation; present but slight

from ± .35 or .40 to ± .60 or .70 substantial or marked rela-tionship

above ± .70 high to very high relationship

The reader is reminded, however, that these are very general estimates and must be interpreted with great caution. Correlation coefficients must always be judged in the light of (1) the size and variability of each of the groups involved, (2) the nature of the variables correlated, (3) the reliabilities of the tests or ratings involved, and (4) the purpose for which the correlation coefficient was computed.

Correlations are used for many purposes. In connection with testing, however, the principal uses of this measure lie in estimating the reliability and validity of tests. Further discussion of corre-lation coefficients with reference to reliability and validity will be found in Chapter 4.

In some test literature the reader may find that the coefficient of correlation has been "corrected for attenuation." Such correction is an attempt to nullify statistically the influence of any unreliability in the two measures involved in a correlation calculation. Although it may be used with other statistical terms, in the present context it probably is most pertinent to coefficients of validity. For example, if scores on a musical aptitude test are correlated with teacher ratings for purposes of validation, the reliability (consistency) of the test and the reliability of the ratings inevitably influence the value of the resulting coefficient. If either scores or ratings are unreliable, the coefficient of correlation between them will be reduced, thus providing an inaccurately low estimate of validity. It is possible, through application of a formula, to estimate what the correlation coefficient would be if the two measures used were perfectly reliable. Hence, a correlation coefficient which has been corrected for attenuation may be assumed to be somewhat higher than it would be had not such a correction been calculated.

Measures of Error

In standardizing measuring instruments and setting up tables of norms it usually is impossible to administer a test to all of the cases in a particular category or population. For example, in attempting to ascertain "normal" performance for fifth grade students on a measure of musical aptitude, ideally one should administer the measure to all students in all fifth grades. Obviously, such a procedure would be quite beyond the limits of practicability. The usual procedure, therefore, is to select sample groups of persons in the category, in this case fifth graders, choosing the samples with care so that they are truly representative of the entire category or population.

Even when the samples are carefully chosen and can be considered truly representative, some question always remains concerning the accuracy of the various statistical measures derived from the work of the sample students. *If* all fifth graders had taken the test would the range of scores, the mean score, etc., have been different from the same measures compiled by the samples, and, if so, how much different? Fortunately, other statistical measures enable us to find out how closely the sample group has approximated the true mean, the true standard deviation, etc., that is, those which would have resulted if *all* students within the category had been measured. These measures are known as *measures of error.*

In modern literature the *standard error* is that most frequently used to indicate how far an obtained statistic may be from the true measure. The standard error may be abbreviated SE or S, or in some contexts it may be represented by the Greek letter sigma (σ). Since S and σ are used also as symbols for the standard deviation, the reader is cautioned against confusing the latter with the standard error. Since a standard error is an error of some statistic, the symbol representing the former, SE or S, will always have a subscript identifying the statistic to which the standard error is being applied. Thus, SE_M and S_M (or, in some literature SE_X or S_X) stand for the standard error of the mean; SE_s and S_s indicate the standard error of the standard deviation.

The meaning of the standard error will be made more clear by an example. If we wished to determine the mean score which would result if a musical aptitude test were administered to all fifth grade students, we probably would give the test to samples of fifth grade students. We then could compute the mean of the scores attained by these sample fifth graders and infer from that what the true mean of the entire population, i.e., all fifth graders, would be. Assume that the mean score derived from the samples' scores is 68 and that SE_M is found to be 3. We can assume, then, within certain limits of probability, that our obtained mean (68) falls within 3 of the true mean. Since the obtained mean may be above or below the true mean, we can say with a certain degree of confidence that the true mean lies somewhere between 65 (68 − 3) and 71 (68 + 3).

This does not imply that the true mean may be any one of the scores within this interval. The true mean of the entire population is a fixed score. The probability referred to is the probability that we are correct in assuming that the true mean falls within a specified range of scores.

Confidence in a statistic, in terms of standard error, commonly is expressed at two levels. These are known as the five per cent level of confidence and the one per cent level of confidence. To make an assumption at the five per cent level of confidence means that the chances are 95 in 100 that the assumption is correct, or, to state this conversely, that the chances are only 5 in 100 that the assumption is not correct. To make an assumption at the one per cent level of confidence means that the chances are 99 in 100 that the assumption is correct, or that the chances are 1 in 100 that it is incorrect.

If we wish to assume at the five per cent level of confidence, we must choose our interval limits at ±1.96 units of standard error from our obtained statistic. In the foregoing example, if we wish to have 95 chances in 100 (or odds of 19 to 1) that we shall be correct, we shall assume that the true population mean falls within the interval bounded by the obtained mean (68) plus 1.96 σ_M (1.96 x 3) and the obtained mean minus 1.96 σ_M. Thus, if we assume that the true mean lies between 62.12 and 73.88, the chances are 95 in 100 that we are right.

If we wish to be more confident that we are right in our assumption, we can widen the interval within which we assume the true mean lies. By setting the interval limits at ±2.58 units of standard error from the statistic, we may assume at the 1 per cent level of confidence, i.e., with chances of 99 in 100 that we are right. In our example, then, if we assume that the true mean lies between 60.26, 68 − (2.58 x 3), and 75.74, 68 + (2.58 x 3), the chances are 99 in 100 that we are right.

Another measure of error may be encountered in some test manuals and other test literature. This is the probable error, abbreviated PE. Some years ago this measure was used quite frequently, but it has been supplanted almost completely by the standard error in more modern usage.

The difference between the standard error and the probable error is one of magnitude only. The probable error is equal to .6745 of the standard error. Due to this difference in size the probabilities given before in terms of units of SE are not accurate for like units of PE. One unit of PE on each side (i.e., above and below) a given statistic gives chances of one in two of finding the true measure, and two units of PE give chances of 82 in 100. Four units of PE give almost certainty, chances of 99.3 in 100.

Thus, if the reader encounters a table or textual material mentioning a mean of 70, with $PE_M = 2$, he can assume, with one chance in two that he is right, that the true mean of the population referred to lies between 68 and 72. If he wishes to have 82 chances in 100 (or odds of about 4.6 to 1) of being right he will assume that the true mean lies between 66 and 74. If he wishes to increase further his chances of being correct, he must widen by additional units of PE_M the interval within which he will assume the true mean falls.

The reader may encounter the use of SE or PE with the coefficient of correlation, i.e., SE_r or PE_r. Some writers on statistics[3] have questioned the use of these measures in estimating the reliability of a coefficient of correlation, since they are based upon assumptions which often are not fulfilled by these coefficients. This is especially true when the number of cases (N) used in computing r is small and when r is either high (.80 or above) or low (.20 or below). For r's closer to .50, and for N's in excess of 100, the use of these measures with r is less likely to be misleading.

The standard error and the probable error estimate only chance errors resulting from the use of samples instead of entire populations. They do not expose errors in computation, nor do they compensate for poor judgment in the selection of the samples. Only careful work can protect the test author or the research worker against these latter sources of error.

Table 1 is taken from a description of reliability of a musical aptitude test battery. It illustrates the manner in which several of the statistical measures discussed in this chapter can be used in test literature.

This table gives the reliability coefficient of a musical aptitude measure with additional statistical information essential for the understanding of this coefficient. N indicates the number of cases

---

[3]See, for example, H. E. Garrett, *Statistics in Psychology and Education.* 5th ed. New York: Longmans, Green, and Co., 1958. p. 199.

Table 1*

Typical Use of Statistical Symbols

Total N	Mean score in %	SD	r	PE_r
1538	69.9	12.9	.79	.02

*Extracted from reliability table in Joseph G. Saetveit, Don Lewis, and Carl E. Seashore, *Revision of the Seashore Measures of Musical Talent.* Iowa City: State University of Iowa Press, 1940. p. 34. Used with the permission of the State University of Iowa.

to whom the test was administered in the reliability study. Scores on this measure are expressed in percentages, and column two shows the mean score attained by this group of 1538 students. *SD* is the standard deviation, and it tells us that 68.26 of the scores fall between 57 per cent (69.9 per cent − 12.9) and 82.8 per cent (69.9 per cent + 12.9); r is the coefficient of reliability of the test. In test manuals or descriptive literature the method used in calculating the reliability of the test usually will be specified. The text accompanying the foregoing table explains that the split half method was used in this case. This method will be described and explained in Chapter 4. In the table PE_r stands for the probable error of the reliability coefficient. It indicates that we may assume, with one chance in two of being correct, that the true r of the population lies between .77 and .81.

Standard Scores

Standard scores give the positions of raw scores in terms of units of standard deviation below or above the mean. The most fundamental form of standard score, also called a z score, arbitrarily assigns the mean of a distribution a standard score value of 0 and the standard deviation a value of 1. Using this scale of standard scores, a raw score lying one unit of standard deviation above the mean would have a standard score of 1; a raw score lying one standard deviation below the mean a standard score value of −1. In a distribution of raw scores with a mean of 76 and a standard deviation of 4, for example, a raw score of 80 would be equivalent to a standard score of 1, a raw score of 72 equivalent to a standard score of −1. In this same distribution, raw scores of 78 and 74 would be equivalent, respectively, to standard scores of .5 and −.5.

To eliminate the use of decimal points and plus and minus signs, other scales of standard scores which assign different values to the mean and standard deviation often are used. Other scales commonly used assign values of 50, 100, or 500 to the mean and values of 10, 20, or 100, respectively, to the standard deviation. Using a mean of 50 and a standard deviation of ten for standard scores, therefore, the raw scores of 72, 74, 78, and 80 used in the foregoing example would be equivalent to standard scores of 40, 45, 55, and 60, respectively. Standard scores using scales such as these, which actually are transformations of z scores, are known also as Z scores.

A slightly different type of standard score may be encountered in some test literature. Designated by the symbol T, these standard scores are derived from the percentile ranks corresponding to the raw scores in a distribution rather than directly from the raw scores themselves. This procedure is somewhat more complicated. The meaning of T scores in test literature is essentially the same as that of z and Z scores; i.e., they indicate distances below and above the mean in terms of standard deviation units, and further explanation is not necessary in the present context. Readers interested in a fuller and more precise understanding of T scores should consult any reliable and up-to-date text on statistics in measurement.

The term *stanines* also may be encountered by the reader of test literature. Stanines are single digit standard scores using a nine point scale with a mean of 5 and a standard deviation of 2.

Standard scores not only show how well an individual has performed in relation to a group, but they also permit comparison of an individual's performance in different fields or on different tests, e.g., music and reading.

SUMMARY

A number of statistical concepts are commonly used in test literature to describe various qualities of tests. Ability to interpret these terms is essential to the understanding of such material. They include norms, measures of central tendency, measures of variability, measures of relationship, and measures of error.

Especially important because of their frequent use are percentile and decile ranks, the mean, the standard deviation, the coefficient of correlation, the standard error, and standard scores.

QUESTIONS FOR DISCUSSION

1. What are the essential differences between a standardized test and an informal teacher-made examination?
2. Why is objectivity an essential characteristic of a standardized test?
3. Explain the difference between norms and standards.
4. What is the significance of a raw score of 75 on a particular test? Of a standing in the 75th percentile rank?
5. Interpret the following table of data concerning a test.

N	M	SD	r	SE_r
175	73	9.7	.88	.03

6. Substitute PE_r of .03 for the SE_r given in the table above, and explain its significance.
7. If the reliability coefficient given above were corrected for attenuation, how would you expect it to be affected, if at all?
8. What factors must be considered in interpreting r?
9. What is the difference in meaning between S and S_M? Explain in detail if M = 70.
10. In a given distribution of raw scores the mean is 82 and the standard deviation 6. Convert to z scores, raw scores of 70, 73, 76, 85, 88, and 94. Convert these same raw scores to standard scores using a scale with a mean of 100 and a standard deviation of 10; using a scale with a mean of 500 and a standard deviation of 100.

RECOMMENDED READINGS

Anastasi, Anne. *Psychological Testing*. 3rd ed. New York: Macmillan, 1968. Chapter 3.

Garrett, Henry E. *Statistics in Psychology and Education.* 5th ed. New York: Longmans, Green, and Co., 1958. Chapters 2, 3, and 8.

Guest Lester. *Beginning Statistics.* New York: Thomas Y. Crowell, 1957. Chapters 3, 4, 6, 7, and 10.

Stanley, Julian C. *Measurement in Today's Schools.* 4th ed. New York: Prentice-Hall, 1964. Chapter 3.

Formulae and Procedures for Computing Basic Statistical Measures

The present chapter may be omitted by those who believe that they can gain an adequate understanding of the basic statistical concepts discussed in Chapter 2 without undertaking actual computations. Those who believe, however, that practice in the use of these measures will strengthen understanding of them will find in this chapter the formulae and procedures used in the computations. It is the author's belief that practice in the computation of the measures will lead to better understanding of them. Furthermore, several of these measures are of great value in scoring informal teacher-made tests and in course grading. The material of the present chapter, then, is pertinent also to the discussions of classroom examinations and course grading which will be found in later chapters.

Frequency Distributions

The first step necessary in computing many basic statistical measures is the arrangement of a set of scores in some kind of order. When a small number of scores is involved, each score may be considered individually, but with a larger number such a procedure is much too cumbersome and laborious. It is usual, therefore, to organize the scores into groups and into a *frequency distribution*.

The first step in grouping scores is the determination of the range of scores, i.e., the numerical interval between the largest and the smallest scores. This is obtained by subtracting the smallest score from the largest. Next, the size of the groups, or class-intervals, must be determined. The size of the class-interval is determined to some extent by the size of the interval between the smallest and the largest scores. Most writers on statistics recommend that scores be grouped in such a way that there are not fewer than ten groups nor more than twenty, although in cases where the range is small fewer than ten groupings sometimes are used. After the range is determined, the size of the class-interval can be chosen by trial and error division of the range by possible interval sizes until the best one is found. In dividing the range by tentative interval sizes, it is well to remember that the quotient obtained will be one less than the number of intervals which will result from the use of a particular interval size. If, for example, a range of 60 is divided by the tentative interval size 5, the resulting quotient is 12. The number of class intervals which would result, then, from the use of intervals of 5 would be 13.

Odd-numbered interval sizes are frequently used since they facilitate the identification of the interval midpoints. The identification of these midpoints is required in the computation of several statistical measures. When the range is large, however, ten is a frequently used interval size.

After the size of the class interval has been determined, the groupings are listed vertically in ascending order from bottom to top. A tabulation of all the scores included is then made by making a tally mark for each to the right of the grouping in which it falls. For ease in handling these figures in subsequent computations, the sum of the tallies beside each grouping is then listed in a column headed *frequency* (f).

An example will clarify this procedure. In Figure 1 are listed scores attained by 64 students on a quiz in Introduction to Music.

88	69	85	96	99	79	73	34
92	89	62	93	87	49	60	61
95	42	97	75	95	77	80	77
59	93	83	100	59	72	73	87
91	97	91	68	94	64	100	70
82	70	73	92	98	95	84	65
101	40	64	79	111	54	81	101
63	73	71	87	72	68	78	43

Figure 1. Scores in Introduction to Music.

Examination of the scores listed in Figure 1 reveals that the largest score is 111 and the smallest 34. To find the range, 34 is subtracted from 111, yielding a difference of 77. Since five often is a convenient size for a class interval, this was used for the first trial grouping. Seventy-seven divided by five yields a quotient of $15\frac{2}{5}$. This quotient actually is one less than the number of class intervals in which an interval of five will result. A class interval of five, then, will result in $16\frac{2}{5}$ groupings or, since partial intervals are not used, 17 groups. Since this is fewer than 20 and more than ten, five can safely be used for the class interval.

The size of the class interval might have been set at seven. This would have yielded 12 groupings ($\frac{77}{7} + 1 = 12$). Nine, also, might have been used. Any odd number smaller than five would result in too many groups, and odd numbers greater than nine would yield intervals of excessive size.

A convenient way of setting up the groups, once the size of the interval is determined, is by starting the lowest group on that multiple of the interval size which falls just below the lowest score. Successive groups then may be laid out, ascending by the chosen interval size until a group which includes the largest score is reached.

The frequency distribution for the set of scores given in Figure 1 is shown in Figure 2.

A few words concerning the description of class intervals are, perhaps, in order. The same interval might be described by different writers in slightly varying terms. The interval 80-84 in the

Class Intervals	Tallies	f
110-114	/	1
105-109		0
100-104	////	4
95- 99	7##/ ///	8
90- 94	7##/ //	7
85- 89	7##/ /	6
80- 84	7##/	5
75- 79	7##/ /	6
70- 74	7##/ ////	9
65- 69	////	4
60- 64	7##/ /	6
55- 59	//	2
50- 54	/	1
45- 49	/	1
40- 44	///	3
35- 39		0
30- 34	/	1

Total 64*

*Totaling of the frequencies serves as a check on the tallying. It also is necessary for subsequent computations.

Figure 2. A frequency distribution of scores in Introduction to Music.

foregoing distribution, for example, actually is considered to extend from 79.5 to 84.5, with the next interval extending from 84.5 to 89.5. Some writers would express the limits of each interval in precisely these terms. A third type of description, used by some, is much less precise. This method would describe the 80-84 interval as 80-85, and the next as 85-90. The overlapping of intervals in this method increases the danger of errors in tabulation, and for this reason it is shunned by many. Thus, different writers might describe the limits of the class intervals in these three different ways. All have the same meaning. The method used in the frequency distribution in Figure 2 seems to be preferred by many writers on statistical methods.

Measures of Central Tendency

The Mean. In an ungrouped distribution, computation of the mean by the simple direct method is quite practicable. The scores are totaled and the sum is divided by the number of scores. This process can be expressed in the simple formula, $M = \dfrac{\Sigma X}{N}$ in which M signifies the mean, ΣX the sum of the scores, and N the number of scores. Σ is the usual symbol for "sum."

With a grouped distribution the procedure is slightly more involved. The formula now is $M = \dfrac{\Sigma fX}{N}$. X now represents the midpoint of each interval, which is taken as the score for that group. f stands for the frequency, or number, of scores in each class-interval. ΣfX is obtained by first multiplying the midpoint of each interval by the number of scores in that group and then totaling the products resulting from this first step.

Figure 3 illustrates the computation of the mean for the distribution given in Figure 2.

The midpoint of an interval is obtained by adding to the actual lower limit of the interval half the actual extent of the interval. Thus, taking an example from the frequency distribution used in Figure 3, the interval 80-84 actually extends from 79.5 up to 84.5. $\dfrac{84.5 - 79.5}{2} = 2.5$. Adding this value to the actual lower limit of our interval (79.5), we obtain 82 as the midpoint.

It might be noted here that if the mean of the 64 scores listed in Figure 1 were computed by the laborious process of adding the ungrouped scores and dividing by N, the mean obtained would be 78.13, a difference of .11 from the mean obtained by formula from the grouped distribution. Small discrepancies of this type, known as *grouping errors*, occur between measures of central tendency and variability calculated from grouped data and those obtained from the same data in an ungrouped distribution. They occur also between measures calculated from distributions using class intervals of different size. Such variations are the result of variations in size and number of groups and of using the midpoint of an interval to represent the value of all scores within that group.

Class Interval Scores	Midpoint X	f	fX
110-114	112	1	112
105-109	107	0	0
100-104	102	4	408
95- 99	97	8	776
90- 94	92	7	644
85- 89	87	6	522
80- 84	82	5	410
75- 79	77	6	462
70- 74	72	9	648
65- 69	67	4	268
60- 64	62	6	372
55- 59	57	2	114
50- 54	52	1	52
45- 49	47	1	47
40- 44	42	3	126
35- 39	37	0	0
30- 34	32	1	32
		N=64	ΣfX=4993

$$M = \frac{\Sigma fX}{N} = \frac{4993}{64} = 78.015 \text{ or } 78.02$$

Figure 3. Computation of the mean from a grouped distribution.

It is possible to apply correction formulae to nullify such discrepancies. In most cases, however, as in the foregoing the discrepancy is so small that it has no practical significance in the type of statistical work with which this chapter is concerned.

A Short Method. One other method of finding the mean of grouped scores deserves attention. This method is especially useful when further calculations, such as of measures of variability and correlation, are to be made. In this method one begins by arbitrarily assuming a mean from an inspection of the data. While there is no set rule to follow in selecting an "assumed mean" (AM), it usually is best to take the midpoint of an interval which appears to be near the center of the distribution. In our sample distribution, 72, the midpoint of the 70-74 interval, might be taken as the assumed mean since this interval seems to be near the center of the distribution. A further indication here is the frequency of scores within that group, since a group with a relatively high frequency and near the center of the distribution usually is a good choice.

We next enter in our table the deviation from the assumed mean of each class interval. This deviation is expressed in terms of units of class interval, and it is positive or negative according to whether the interval falls above or below the AM. In Figure 4 following, the column headed x' lists these deviations. Next, the

Class Intervals	X	f	Deviations from AM x'*	fx'	
110-114	112	1	8	8	
105-109	107	0	7	0	
100-104	102	4	6	24	
95- 99	97	8	5	40	
90- 94	92	7	4	28	
85- 89	87	6	3	18	
80- 84	82	5	2	10	
75- 79	77	6	1	6	+134
70- 74	72	9	0	0	
65- 69	67	4	–1	– 4	
60- 64	62	6	–2	–12	
55- 59	57	2	–3	– 6	
50- 54	52	1	–4	– 4	
45- 49	47	1	–5	– 5	
40- 44	42	3	–6	–18	
35- 39	37	0	–7	0	
30- 34	32	1	–8	–8	– 57
		N = 64			= +77

AM (assumed mean) $= 72$

ci $= + 6.015$

M $= 78.015$ or 78.02

c (correction in class interval units) $= \dfrac{77}{64} = 1.203$

i (size of class interval) $= 5$

ci $= 6.015$

*The diacritical mark indicates the use of an assumed mean and that the deviations, therefore, are from an assumed mean rather than from a true mean.

Figure 4. Computation of the Mean by the Short Method.

deviation of each interval is multiplied by the frequency of scores within that group. The column headed fx' in Figure 4 lists these values, the products of the f column multiplied by the x' column. The fx' column then is totaled algebraically. Division of the algebraic sum of these products by the number of scores results in the *correction*, in units of class interval, for the assumed mean. This correction is converted into score units by multiplying it by the size of the class interval. The correction then is added to or subtracted from the assumed mean, depending upon whether the correction is a plus or a minus value, to provide the true mean.

Figure 4 shows the calculation by this method of the mean of the distribution used in the foregoing examples.

Summarizing these steps with reference to Figure 4, the procedure for finding the mean by the short method is as follows:

(1) Assume a mean (preferably the midpoint of an interval near the middle of the distribution and with a relatively large frequency). AM = 72.

(2) Find the deviation of the midpoint of each class interval from the assumed mean in terms of class interval (column x').

(3) Multiply the deviation (x') of each interval by the number of scores in that interval (f). (column fx'). Retain + and − signs.

(4) Find the algebraic total of fx'. (It is easiest to add the + values and the − values separately, and then to add these two sums algebraically.) In Figure 4 this sum is 77.

(5) Divide the algebraic sum of the frequency-deviation products by the number of scores (N). The quotient obtained is the correction in units of class interval (c). $\dfrac{77}{64} = 1.203$

(6) Multiply the correction (c) by the class interval size. The product obtained is the correction in score units (ci). 1.203 x 5 = 6.015

(7) If ci is a plus value, add it to the assumed mean to obtain the true mean. If ci is a minus value, subtract it from the assumed mean. 72 + 6.015 = 78.015

The Median. The median is the midpoint in a distribution of scores. If the distribution contains an odd number of scores, the median will be an actual score in the distribution. If, however, the distribution contains an even number of scores, the median will be a point lying between the two halves of the distribution. This has been illustrated in Chapter 2.

A formula for finding the median of an ungrouped distribution of scores may be stated as follows:

$$\text{Mdn.} = \text{the } \frac{(N+1)}{2} \text{ th score in order of size}$$

In a distribution containing 11 scores, for example, the median would fall on the sixth score $(\frac{11+1}{2})$, counting from either the bottom or the top of the series. If the series contained 12 scores, the median would fall on the 6½th score $(\frac{12+1}{2})$, or midway between the sixth and seventh scores.

When scores have been grouped in a frequency distribution, the formula for finding the median is:

$$\text{Mdn.} = l + \frac{\left(\frac{N}{2} - F\right)}{f_m} \text{ x i}$$

In this formula l stands for the lower limit of the class interval in which the median lies; $\frac{N}{2}$ = half the number of scores; F = the sum of all the scores below l; f_m = the frequency of scores within the interval which contains the median; and i stands for the size of the class interval.

Application of this formula to the data used for the previous examples may be illustrated with reference back to Figure 3. Since there are 64 scores in the distribution, the median will be the 32.5th score; i.e., it will fall midway between the 32nd and the 33rd scores. By adding the frequencies of the class intervals up to and including 70-74 we find that there are 27 scores included in the intervals. This is 5.5 scores short of the median which must lie, therefore, within the next interval, 75-79. Substituting in the

formula Mdn. $= l + \frac{\left(\frac{N}{2} - F\right)}{f_m}$ x i, we have Mdn. $= 74.5 + \frac{\left(\frac{64}{2} - 27\right)}{6}$

x 5 = 78.7. The reader is reminded that the actual limits of the class interval 75-79 are 74.5 and 79.5.

The steps in finding the median of a grouped distribution may be summarized as follows:

(1) Divide the number of scores in the distribution by 2.

(2) Count off the scores in order, beginning at the lower end of the distribution, until reaching the lower limit of the interval which contains the median. The result of this count is used as F in the formula.

(3) Calculate the number of scores needed to make up half the total number, i.e., $\frac{N}{2}$.

(4) Subtract F from $\frac{N}{2}$.

(5) Divide the difference obtained in step 4 by the frequency of scores found in the interval containing the median (f_m).

(6) Multiply the quotient obtained in step 5 by the size of the class interval (i).

(7) Add the product obtained in step 6 to the lower limit of the interval which contains the median. Remember to use the actual lower limit of the interval. The sum obtained in this step is the median of the distribution.

Measures of Variability

The Standard Deviation. The standard deviation, abbreviated σ or SD, may be defined as the square root of the mean of the squared deviations from the mean of the distribution. When the scores in the distribution are not grouped, this definition may be expressed in the formula $\sigma = \sqrt{\frac{\Sigma x^2}{N}}$; in which σ stands for the standard deviation, Σx^2 the sum of the squared deviations of the several scores from the arithmetic mean, and N the number of scores in the distribution.

When scores are grouped in a frequency distribution, each squared deviation from the mean must be weighted, or multiplied, by the frequency of scores within the interval which the deviation represents. The formula for the standard deviation then becomes $\sigma = \sqrt{\frac{\Sigma f x^2}{N}}$.

The procedure for calculating the standard deviation for grouped distributions by use of the foregoing formula involves the use of rather cumbersome quantities. Another method, involving the use of an assumed mean, avoids the use of these cumbersome figures, although the formula itself is slightly more complex. Since this latter method is preferable in many cases, an illustration of it, using the data already described in previous examples, will be given first. The formula used for this "Short Method" of computing the standard deviation is $\sigma = \sqrt{\dfrac{\Sigma fx'^2}{N}} - c^2$ x i. In this formula c^2

Class Intervals	X	f	x'	fx'	fx'²
110-114	112	1	8	8	64
105-109	107	0	7	0	0
100-104	102	4	6	24	144
95- 99	97	8	5	40	200
90- 94	92	7	4	28	112
85- 89	87	6	3	18	54
80- 84	82	5	2	10	20
75- 79	77	6	1	6	6
70- 74	72	9	0	0	0
65- 69	67	4	-1	- 4	4
60- 64	62	6	-2	-12	24
55- 59	57	2	-3	- 6	18
50- 54	52	1	-4	- 4	16
45- 49	47	1	-5	- 5	25
40- 44	42	3	-6	-18	108
35- 39	37	0	-7	0	0
30- 34	32	1	-8	- 8	64
		N=64		+77	859

$AM = 72$ $\quad$ $c = 1.203$ $\quad$ $\sigma = \sqrt{\dfrac{\Sigma fx'^2}{N}} - c^2$ $\quad$ x i

$ci = 6.015$ $\quad$ $c^2 = 1.447$ $\quad$ $\sigma = \sqrt{\dfrac{859}{64}} - 1.447$ x 5 = 17.30

$M = 78.015$ or 78.02

Figure 5. Computation of the standard deviation by the Short Method.

stands for the square of the correction of the assumed mean, and i stands for the size of the class interval. The other symbols have the same meaning as in the simpler formula given before.

The reader doubtless has noticed that all of the steps used in calculating the true mean by the Short Method, except the direct calculation of ci, are needed in computing the standard deviation by the Short Method. In filling out the fx'^2 column, which results from multiplying each value in the fx' column by its corresponding value in the x' column, the minus signs are lost since a negative value multiplied by another negative value results in a positive number.

For purposes of comparison, calculation of the standard deviation of the same set of scores by the "Long Method" is given in Figure 6. The procedure in general is very much like that used in the "Short Method." The difference is that in the Long Method the true mean is used and the deviations of the scores, therefore, are deviations from the true mean instead of from an assumed mean. This results in the more cumbersome figures in the last three columns.

The Quartile Deviation. Although used less frequently than the standard deviation, the quartile deviation (Q) may be of value in some situations. The quartile deviation is defined as one half of the distance between the first quartile and the third quartile. These two points are defined, respectively, as that point below which fall 25 per cent of the scores in a distribution, and that point below which fall 75 per cent of the scores. The formula for calculating the quartile deviation, then, is $Q = \dfrac{Q_3 - Q_1}{2}$.

Q_3 and Q_1 may be found in a grouped distribution by a procedure similar to that used to find the median. To find Q_1, count off 25 per cent of the scores in the distribution, starting from the bottom. In our sample distribution, 25 per cent of the total number of scores (64) is 16 scores. Counting from the lower end of the distribution, we find that the first seven class intervals contain 14 scores. The next interval, 65-69, contains four, of which we need two to reach Q_1. ($\dfrac{2}{4}$ x 5) + 64.5, the lower limit of the 65-69 interval, will fill out the lowest 25 per cent of the scores in the distribution. Q_1, therefore, is 67.

Class Intervals	X	f	x	fx	fx^2
110-114	112	1	33.98	33.98	1154.64
105-109	107	0	28.88	00.00	00.00
100-104	102	4	23.88	95.92	2300.16
95- 99	97	8	18.98	151.84	2881.92
90- 94	92	7	13.98	97.86	1368.08
85- 89	87	6	8.98	53.88	483.84
80- 84	82	5	3.98	19.90	78.20
75- 79	77	6	− 1.02	− 6.12	6.24
70- 74	72	9	− 6.02	− 54.18	326.16
65- 69	67	4	−11.02	− 44.08	485.76
60- 64	62	6	−16.02	− 96.12	1539.84
55- 59	57	2	−21.02	− 42.04	883.68
50- 54	52	1	−26.02	− 26.02	677.04
45- 49	47	1	−31.02	− 31.02	962.24
40- 44	42	3	−36.02	−108.06	3892.32
35- 39	37	0	−41.02	00.00	00.00
30- 34	32	1	−46.02	− 46.02	2117.84
		N=64			19157.96

$$SD = \sqrt{\frac{\Sigma fx^2}{N}} = \sqrt{\frac{19157.96}{64}} = 17.38$$

Figure 6. Computation of the standard deviation by the Long Method.

To find Q_3, count off 75 per cent of the scores in the distribution. 75 per cent of 64 scores is equal to 48 scores. Counting from the bottom, we find 44 scores in the intervals up to and including the 85-89 interval. The next interval, 90-94, contains seven scores, of which four are needed to fill out the lowest 75 per cent of the distribution. Following the same procedure as that used to find Q_1, Q_3 is found to be 92.76.

Substituting in the formula $Q = \frac{Q_3 - Q_1}{2}$, we have $Q = \frac{92.76 - 67}{2}$ or 12.88.

The Mean Deviation. The mean deviation (MD), also called the average deviation (AD) and the mean variation (MV), is the mean of the deviations of the several scores in a series taken from their central tendency, usually the mean. The formula for finding the MD of an ungrouped distribution is MD $= \dfrac{\Sigma \, ||x||}{N}$. The vertical bars surrounding x indicate that plus and minus signs are disregarded in obtaining the sum of the deviations. Since x stands for the deviation of each score from the mean, the procedure consists of adding these deviations and dividing the sum by the number of scores in the distribution. Thus, in the series 10, 12, 15, 18, 25, the mean is 16. Deviations from the mean are respectively, –6, –4, –1, 2, 9. $\Sigma \, ||x|| = 22$, and MD $= 4.4$.

The formula for finding the MD from grouped data is MD $= \dfrac{\Sigma \, ||fx||}{N}$. Since the procedure requires several of the same steps that are used in finding the SD by the Long Method, it may be described with reference to Figure 6. The procedures are identical up through the derivation of the fx column. First, the deviation of each score interval (as represented by its midpoint) from the true mean is computed. Then each deviation is multiplied by the number of scores in its class interval. This step results in the fx column. This column then is totaled without regard for the plus and minus signs. The sum of the fx column in Figure 6 is 907.04. Substituting in the formula, then, we have MD $= \dfrac{907.04}{64} = 14.17$.

The mean deviation also may be calculated from an assumed mean by a "short" method. Since the MD is not frequently used, and since this "short" method is neither really short nor really satisfactory, it will not be given here.

Percentile Ranks

The reader may wish to divide a distribution into percentile ranks. The procedure used previously to find the median, Q_1, and Q_3 may be applied to this purpose also. Thus, to find the score which would stand in the 40th percentile rank in our sample distribution, we first must calculate how many scores comprise the bottom 40 per cent of the series. Forty per cent of 64 scores is 25.6 scores. Counting from the bottom of the distribution we find that the first eight class intervals contain 18 scores.

The ninth interval, 70-74, contains nine scores of which we need 7.6 to fill out the bottom 40 per cent of the distribution. Multiplying $\frac{7.6}{9}$ x 5, the interval size, and adding the result to 69.5, the lower limit of the interval 70-74, we find that a score of 73.7 stands in the 40th percentile rank.

If one wishes to find the percentile rank for a particular score, he must follow the reverse procedure. In this case the percentage of the distribution which falls below the specified score must be found. This can be illustrated with reference to the sample distribution used in the previous illustrations. If we wish to find the percentile rank in this distribution of the score 63, we first locate this score in the class interval 60-64. We find that eight scores lie below this class interval. There are six scores in this interval, and by dividing six by five, the size of the interval, we find that each unit of class interval includes 1.2 scores. By subtracting the lower limit of the interval, 59.5, from our score, 63, we find that this score falls 3.5 score units from the lower limit of the interval. Multiplying 1.2 by 3.5 we get 4.2 as the score distance of our score, 63, from the lower limit, 59.5. By adding 4.2 to 8, the number of scores falling below the interval 60-64, we find that 12.2 scores of the 64 in the distribution lie below the score 63. Converting this number into a percentage of the distribution, we find that 19 per cent of the distribution lies below the score 63 and that, therefore, this score stands in the 19th percentile rank.

Measures of Relationship

The Rank Difference Method. The rank difference method of estimating correlation is useful when small numbers of scores are involved. It requires less complicated computations than the product-moment method and, although it is less accurate than the latter in that it does not take into account the magnitude of scores and of the differences between them, it provides indications of relationship adequate for many purposes.

To obtain a coefficient of correlation by the rank-difference method, one first lists the two sets of scores or measures. Ranks then are assigned to the scores or measures in each set. The differences between ranks then are obtained by subtracting one from the other, and these differences are squared. The squared differences are added next, and the sum obtained is substituted in the formula ρ (rho) $= 1 - \dfrac{6(\Sigma D^2)}{N(N^2-1)}$.

Figure 7 illustrates the computation by the rank-difference method of a coefficient of correlation for scores attained on two different tests by 19 students in a course in History and Literature of Music.

The procedure for finding the coefficient of correlation by the rank-difference method can be summarized in the following steps:

(1) List the two sets of scores or measures to be correlated. These need not be listed in order of magnitude, but they should be properly paired.

(2) Assign each score in each list a rank.

(3) Find the difference between rankings by subtracting the rank for set 2 from that for set 1.

(4) Square the difference between ranks.

(5) Add the squared differences and substitute this sum (ΣD^2) and the number of cases (N) in the formula.

The Product-Moment Method. When large numbers of scores are to be correlated, or when a more exact estimate of correlation is desired, the product-moment method is preferable to the rank-difference method just described. The usual method of computing a product-moment coefficient of correlation when large numbers of scores are involved makes use of a *scatter diagram,* or *scattergram* as it is also called. This is a kind of two-way frequency chart. One set of scores is laid out vertically along the left hand margin of the scattergram, ranging from bottom to top in order of size. The other set of scores is laid out across the top margin, with low scores at the left and high scores at the right of the diagram. Figure 8 shows a scattergram in which the scores used for the computations of the measures of central tendency and the foregoing measures of variability have been correlated with scores attained by the same students on another Introduction to Music quiz.

Student	Scores		Ranks		D	D²
	Test 1	Test 2	Test 1	Test 2		
A	51	51	3.0	6.0	− 3.0	9.00
B	41	50	11.5*	7.5*	4.0	16.00
C	31	23	18.0	18.0	0.0	0.00
D	47	55	6.0	4.0	2.0	4.00
E	27	19	19.0	19.0	0.0	0.00
F	38	56	15.5	2.5	13.0	169.00
G	36	41	17.0	11.5	5.5	30.25
H	41	31	11.5	17.0	− 5.5	30.25
I	42	37	9.5	14.0	− 4.5	20.25
J	40	33	13.0	16.0	− 3.0	9.00
K	46	42	7.5	10.0	− 2.5	6.25
L	49	40	4.0	13.0	− 9.0	81.00
M	61	65	1.0	1.0	0.0	0.00
N	39	41	14.0	11.5	2.5	6.25
O	42	43	9.5	9.0	.5	.25
P	46	56	7.5	2.5	5.0	25.00
Q	38	36	15.5	15.0	.5	.25
R	48	50	5.0	7.5	− 2.5	6.25
S	56	54	2.0	5.0	− 3.0	9.00

N = 19   422.00

$$\text{rho} = 1 - \frac{6(\Sigma D^2)}{N(N^2-1)} = 1 - \frac{2532}{6840} = .63$$

*In ranking, when two or more persons attain the same score, they all are assigned the mean of the ranks which they would occupy had their scores been contiguous but not identical. On Test 1 above, for example, students K and P both scored 46. Score 47 is in rank 6, so K and P share ranks 7 and 8, and both are assigned rank 7.5, the mean of ranks 7 and 8.

Figure 7. Computation of a coefficient of correlation by the Rank-Difference Method.

Inspection of a scattergram will yield a quick, if rough, estimate of the degree of correlation between the two sets of scores. If the correlation is positive and high, the entries in the scattergram will tend to cluster along a diagonal running from lower left to upper right. If the correlation is negative and high, they will tend to cluster along a diagonal running from lower right to upper left.

The lower the degree of correlation, the more the entries will deviate from both of these tendencies and scatter over the diagram.

In the scattergram shown in Figure 8 there is some tendency for the entries to group along a diagonal from lower left to upper right, indicating some positive correlation. With this tendency, however, there also is some scattering. The correlation coefficient found for these two sets of scores was .52.

Scores are entered in the scattergram in the following manner. The first student listed in the sample group attained a score of 88 on quiz 1 and a score of 85 on quiz 2. Finding the square on the diagram which lies to the right of the 85-89 class interval in the left margin (quiz 1 scores) and beneath the 85-89 class interval at the top (quiz 2 scores), we first make a tally mark. The next student attained a score of 92 on quiz 1 and a score of 85 on quiz 2. This time a tally mark is placed in the box which lies to the right of the 90-94 class interval in the left margin and beneath the 85-89 class interval in the top margin. This procedure is continued until all pairs of scores have been entered. It is advisable then to total the number of tally marks in each box. In Figure 8 tally marks have been entered in the upper left hand corner of each box. The frequency of tallies in each box is represented by the number in the center of the box.

The formula used for calculating a coefficient of correlation by the scattergram method is $r = \dfrac{\dfrac{\Sigma fd'_x d'_y}{N} - c_x c_y}{\sigma_x \sigma_y}$.[1]

The information needed for the solution of this formula is gathered from the columns which appear at the right of the scattergram and from the rows at the bottom. The derivation of this information can be described best by outlining the steps necessary to the filling out of these columns and rows.

(1) After the scores have been tallied and the tallies in each box have been totaled, the f_y column is filled out by summing the tallies across each row of boxes. In Figure 8, to the right of score interval 95-99, we find a total of eight

---

[1]σ_x and σ_y in this context stand for the standard deviations of the two distributions of test scores. They do not stand for the standard error. The subscripts are not symbols used to represent specific statistical measures.

tallies. Eight is entered, therefore, beside that row in the f_y column. The f_x row at the bottom of the diagram is filled out in a similar manner by totaling tallies vertically.

(2) The column d'_y represents the deviations in terms of class interval units of the score groups on quiz 1 from the assumed mean of those scores. Similarly, d'_x represents deviations from the assumed mean of the scores on quiz 2. The procedure for deriving these deviations has been described in connection with the computation of the standard deviation by the short method.

(3) The procedure for filling out the columns and rows headed fd'_x, fd'_y, fd'^2_x, and fd'^2_y is obvious. These, too, have been used in the computation of the standard deviation. They are used here to provide c_x, c_y, σ_x and σ_y. Since all deviations are expressed in terms of class interval units, c_x, c_y, σ_x, and σ_y are left in terms of class interval units in solving the formula.

(4) The column headed $fd'_x\, d'_y$ represents a step which has not been used in earlier computations. The first step in the calculation of the values for the $fd'_x d'_y$ column is the finding of a *product-deviation* for each of the boxes of tallies in the diagram. This product-deviation is obtained by multiplying the y deviation of the box by its x deviation. Taking as an example the box in Figure 8 which lies to the right of class interval 100-104 and beneath class interval 95-99, we find that its y deviation is 6 and its x deviation 5. Multiplying these two values results in a product-deviation of 30 for this box. This number has been written in the upper right hand corner of the box, as have the product-deviations for the other boxes. Each product-deviation then must be weighted by the number of score tallies in its box. The weighted product-deviations then are added algebraically across the diagram, and the algebraic sum of each row of boxes is entered in the $fd'_x d'_y$ column. In Figure 8 to the right of class interval 75-79, for example, we find a product-deviation of -4 with a frequency of 1, a product-deviation of 0 with a frequency of 1, a product-deviation of 1 with a frequency of 3, and a product-deviation of 4 with a frequency of 1. Weighting each product-deviation by its

	35–39	40–44	45–49	50–54	55–59	60–64	65–69	70–74	75–79	80–84	85–89	90–94	95–99	100–104	f_y	d'_y	fd'_y	fd'^2_y	fd_xd_y
110–114								AM=72					1 ⁴⁰		1	8	8	64	40
105–109															0	7	0	0	0
100–104						1 ⁻¹²			1 ⁶		1 ¹⁸		1 ³⁰		4	6	24	144	42
95–99			1 1 ⁻²⁵			1 ⁻¹⁰	1 1 ⁻⁴		1 ⁴	1 ¹⁰	1 ¹⁵ 2 ²⁰	2 ²⁰	2 ²⁵	1 1 ²⁴	8	5	40	200	80
90–94							1 1 ⁻³		1 ⁴	1 ⁸ 2 ¹²	2 ¹²		1 1 ¹⁵		7	4	28	112	56
85–89						1 1 ⁻⁴			1 ⁶	1 1 1 3 ⁹	1 1 1 3 ⁹	1 ⁴			6	3	18	54	45
80–84				1 1 ⁻⁴				1 1 2 0 1	1 1 2 0 1	1 ⁴					5	2	10	20	2
75–79	AM=72		1 1 ⁰ 1					1 1 0 1 1 1 3	1 1 1 3 ⁰	0 1 1 ³	0 1 1 ²	1 1 ⁴			6	1	6	6	3
70–74				1 1 ⁴				1 1 0	1 1 0 1	0 1	0 1 1 2 ⁰				9	0	0	0	0
65–69					1 1 ⁶		1 1 2 ¹	1 1 ⁰	1 1 ⁻² 1 1	1 1 2 ⁻⁴					4	−1	−4	4	6
60–64				1 1 ⁴			1 1 2 ¹	1 1 ⁰	1 1 ⁻²	2 ⁻³					6	−2	−12	24	−2
55–59					1 1 ¹²										2	−3	−6	18	−6
50–54					1 1 ¹²										1	−4	−4	16	12
45–49							1 1 ⁵								1	−5	−5	25	5
40–44	1 1 ⁴²					1 1 ¹²									3	−6	−18	108	78
35–39															0	−7	0	0	0
30–34						1 1 ¹⁶									1	−8	−8	64	16
f_x	1	0	2	4	2	5	6	7	12	7	9	3	5	1	64		+77	859	377
d'_x	−7	−6	−5	−4	−3	−2	−1	0	1	2	3	4	5	6					
fd'_x	−7	0	−10	−16	−6	−10	−6	0	12	14	27	12	25	6	+41				
fd'^2_x	49	0	50	64	18	20	6	0	12	28	81	48	125	36	537				

$c_x = .640*$

$c_y = 1.203*$

$\sigma_x = 2.82*†$

$\sigma_y = 3.46*†$

$$r = \frac{\dfrac{\Sigma fd'_x d'_y}{N} - c_x c_y}{\sigma_x \sigma_y}$$

$$r = \frac{\dfrac{377}{64} - (.64 \times 1.203)}{2.82 \times 3.46} = .52$$

*Since all product-deviations ($fd'_x d'_y$'s) are in terms of class interval units, c_x, c_y, σ_x, and σ_y are left in terms of class intervals.

†σ_x and σ_y stand for the SD's of the two tests.

c_x is the correction for the assumed mean of the horizontal distribution $\left(\dfrac{fd_x}{f_x}\right)$.

c_y is the correction for the assumed mean of the vertical distribution $\left(\dfrac{fd_y}{f_y}\right)$.

Figure 8. Computation of a Product–Moment Coefficient of Correlation by the Scatter-gram Method.

54

frequency and adding algebraically across the row, we obtain an algebraic sum of 3, which is entered opposite that row in the fd′$_x$d′$_y$ column.

(5) The fd′$_x$d′$_y$ column then is totaled algebraically. All of the information needed for the solution of the formula now is available.

Measures of Error

The Standard Error. Since a measure of error always is applied to some other statistic, formulae for these measures can be expressed best with reference to specific statistical measures. The formula for finding the standard error of the mean (SE$_M$ or σ_M), therefore, is $SE_M = \dfrac{\sigma}{\sqrt{N}}$, in which σ stands for the standard deviation of the population and N for the number of cases in the sample used. Since the standard deviation of the population usually is not available, the best substitute available, which is the standard deviation of the sample used, takes the place of the former in the formula.

If the sample used is small, i.e., contains fewer than 50 cases, a modified formula should be used in computing the standard error. The modified formula for the standard error of the mean is $SE_M = \dfrac{\sigma}{\sqrt{N-1}}$. The same modification should be made in each of the formulas following when the sample used is small. Use of the modified formula is safe in any case since when N is large the modification results in a negligible difference.

The standard error of the median (SE$_{Mdn}$ or σ_{Mdn}) can be computed from either the standard deviation or the quartile deviation. The formula for the former, when N is large, is $\sigma_{Mdn} = \dfrac{1.253\sigma}{\sqrt{N}}$. Using the quartile deviation the formula becomes $\sigma_{Mdn} = \dfrac{1.858Q}{\sqrt{N}}$.

To find the standard error of the standard deviation (SE$_\sigma$ or σ_σ) when the group is large, the formula is as follows: $SE_\sigma = \dfrac{.707\sigma}{\sqrt{N}}$.

The standard error of the quartile deviation (σ_Q or SE$_Q$) can be found with the formula $SE_Q = \dfrac{.787\sigma}{\sqrt{N}}$ or, using the quartile deviation, $SE_Q = \dfrac{1.166Q}{\sqrt{N}}$.

With large samples the standard error of the coefficient of correlation can be found with the formula $SE_r = \dfrac{(1\text{-}r^2)}{\sqrt{N}}$. The reader is reminded of the objections of some writers to the use of the standard error or the probable error with the coefficient of correlation. These objections have been discussed briefly in Chapter 2.

The Probable Error. Since the probable error $= .6745$ of the standard error, any of the formulae given before can be converted to a formula for the probable error of the statistic involved by adding this multiplier. The formula for PE_M, for example, becomes

$$PE_M = .6745\left(\frac{\sigma}{\sqrt{N}}\right).$$

Problems for Practice.

1. Arrange the following list of scores in a grouped frequency distribution and compute the mean, the median, the standard deviation, the quartile deviation, and the mean deviation.

80	91	93	59	96	90	84	79	107	81
107	60	81	107	97	81	53	71	92	71
92	71	97	56	44	64	44	80	66	51
69	104	78	92	72	70	96	88	82	66
69	43	101	65	70	87	77	61	78	81

2. In the foregoing series of scores, find the percentile rank for a score of 65; a score of 97. In this same series of scores find Q_1 and Q_3.

3. Make out a scattergram and calculate a product-moment coefficient of correlation between the series of scores given in Question 1 and the series which follows.

88	93	64	87	64	92	97	71	95	95
95	70	96	59	54	59	40	93	94	68
91	73	75	98	73	82	85	100	111	60
101	62	68	72	80	63	97	92	79	73
69	83	79	49	100	89	91	87	77	84

4. Calculate a rank-difference coefficient of correlation between the two sets of scores which follow.

	Set A			Set B	
93	64	87	69	92	107
97	71	95	51	71	79
70	96	59	82	66	53
40	93	94	80	81	90
73	75	98	44	97	96

RECOMMENDED READINGS

The number of statistics texts currently available is far too great to permit the listing here of even a substantial portion. The following, in the author's opinion, are up-to-date and reliable sources. This does not imply that there are not many others which will provide information as good for the purposes of the reader of this book.

Downie, N. M. and Heath, R. W. *Basic Statistical Methods.* New York: Harper and Bros., 1959.

Garrett, H. E. *Statistics in Psychology and Education.* 5th ed. New York: Longmans, Green, and Co., 1958.

Guest, Lester. *Beginning Statistics.* New York: Thomas Y. Crowell, 1957.

Mack, Sidney F. *Elementary Statistics.* New York: Henry Holt, 1960.

CHAPTER 4

What to Look for in a Test

In selecting or constructing a test for use in a particular situation, or even in determining the general value of any test, one must consider a number of criteria. Some of these might be called technical in nature and are common to all tests. These criteria usually are evaluated by statistical means and they have the same general significance in any situation. Foremost among these technical criteria are *validity* and *reliability*.

Other criteria tend to be matters of practicality in a particular situation, or where a specific purpose is intended. The importance of any one of these may vary from one situation to another, although many of them are common to most testing occasions.

In general many of the same qualities are of consequence in informal teacher-made tests as in standardized published measures. Knowledge of the significance of these qualities, and of how to estimate their presence, obviously is essential to an understanding of tests and testing.

Reliability

One of the most important qualities of any test is *reliability.* This, in essence, is the consistency of the test. Can the results realized by any test be accepted as a true estimate of what a particular subject is able to do on that test? If he were to take the same test or an equivalent test at different times would the results obtained be substantially the same? If not, the test is unreliable.

The importance of reliability in a test is obvious. If a test yields widely varying results in different administrations to the same subject, which result can be considered the true estimate of that subject's ability? There is no way of knowing.

Reliability of a test usually is estimated by statistical methods, and most frequently it is expressed by means of a coefficient of correlation. One method commonly used by test authors to estimate the reliability of a test is the so-called *test-retest* method. As the name implies, this consists of administering the same test to the same subject or group of subjects at different times. The two sets of scores then are correlated, and the resulting coefficient is taken as the measure of the reliability of the test.

Like the other procedures used to establish the reliability of a test, the retest method has certain limitations and is vulnerable to specific criticisms. If the period of time which elapses between testings is of any length, maturation may affect the results obtained. Certainly, if practice or any learning which might affect results on the test takes place in the period between testings, the estimate of reliability obtained by the retest method inevitably will be compromised. Some critics hold that if the retest takes place soon after the original testing, on the other hand, familiarity with the test will affect results. Since all subjects will not benefit equally from such familiarity, they contend, the estimate of reliability again will not be as accurate as one might wish. When testings are close together a subject may remember specific items of the test and the answers which he made to them. This frequently will lead to a repetition of the same answers solely because those answers were given the first time rather than because the subject reaches the same conclusion upon two different occasions. This results in a spurious consistency and an artifically high estimate of reliability for the test.

Another common procedure is the so-called *parallel forms* or *equivalent forms* method. This method requires the use of two different but equivalent forms of the same test. The two forms are administered to the same group of subjects, and the two sets of scores are correlated. The resulting coefficient gives an estimate of the reliability of the test.

The principal limitation of this method is the difficulty of making two forms of a test which measure the same characteristics and are equivalent in difficulty, yet which do not overlap in content. If the two forms are not truly equivalent, the correlation between the two sets of scores will underestimate the reliability of the test. Overlapping, on the other hand, will result in a spuriously high coefficient of reliability. Another difficulty inherent in this method when used with certain types of tests is the practice or experience factor. If the test presents to the subject a task which is unique and unfamiliar to him, the experience gained in taking the first form of the test may be a significant factor in raising his score on the alternate form. The result then would be an underestimation of the reliability of the test.

A method which averts some of the criticisms of the retest method and eliminates the difficulties encountered in constructing alternate forms of a test is the so-called *split-half* method. In this procedure only a single form of a test need be prepared and administered. In scoring, the test then is divided into halves, half the items of the test going into one division and the remainder into the other. Various methods are used to divide tests into halves for this purpose. Perhaps the most common, used when test items are arranged in order of difficulty, is the odd-even division. By placing all odd numbered items in one division and all even numbered items in the other, it can best be ensured with a test of this type that the two halves will be equivalent in difficulty. Such equivalency is essential in the use of the split-half method. If test items are grouped according to content or difficulty, division by alternate groups may be preferable. Under some circumstances the first half of the test may be separated from the second half. The arrangement of the items in the whole test will determine the best method of dividing the test into halves for purposes of estimating reliability. The essential requirement is that the two halves be equivalent.

After the test has been divided into halves, scores for each of the two halves are computed and these scores then are correlated. This procedure gives the reliability of the half test. Application of the Spearman-Brown formula, a statistical device first presented by Spearman in 1910, then results in an estimation of reliability for the whole test.

The split-half method of estimating test reliability is widely used by test authors. Its principal limitation lies in the type of test with which it is used. With any test in which speed is a significant factor in the scores attained by any group of subjects, use of the split-half technique is inappropriate and lacking in meaning. Thorndike, discussing test reliability in *Educational Measurement*,[1] has stated that split-half estimates of reliability for speeded tests are, in general, misleadingly high and that split-half estimates, even with unspeeded tests, tend to err on the high side.

Another method of estimating reliability from a single testing and a single test form was devised by Kuder and Richardson.[2] This technique is based upon analysis of the performance of the trial subjects on each item in the test. It actually yields, therefore, an estimate of inter-item consistency. The type of reliability estimate produced by the Kuder-Richardson method has characteristics similar to that obtained from split-half procedures, and, according to Thorndike[3], it is subject to some of the same limitations. It, too, is inappropriate for use with any test in which speed is a significant factor.

Which method of determining reliability is best depends largely upon the situation or upon the test involved. No one method can be said to be superior in general. For this reason knowledge of the method used in deriving the reliability coefficient of a test, and of the circumstances of the study through which that coefficient was derived, are important to the understanding and evaluation of that measure.

Reliability and reliability coefficients are affected by a number of factors. The length of a test has considerable influence upon

---

[1]E. F. Lindquist (ed.), *Educational Measurement*. Washington, D.C.: American Council on Education, 1951. p. 583.

[2]G. F. Kuder and M. W. Richardson, "The Theory of Estimation of Test Reliability," *Psychometrika*, 2, 1937. pp. 151-60.

[3]E. F. Lindquist (ed.), op. cit., pp. 587-8.

its reliability. In general, a higher degree of reliability may be expected from a fairly long measure than from a short one, although beyond a certain limit boredom and fatigue may become influential. Too short a test does not provide an adequate sampling of the subject's abilities, and the score is more strongly influenced by guessing. In this connection, it should be kept in mind that length of a test is measured not only by the number of items included but also by the number of response options given in each item. A set of multiple choice items, for example, should prove more reliable in general than an equal number of true-false items provided that the options in the multiple choice items are equivalent in difficulty. Other characteristics of a test may, of course, compensate for its length.

The variability of the group tested also is significant in estimating the reliability of a test or in evaluating its reliability coefficient. In general, a smaller reliability coefficient is to be expected when a relatively homogeneous group is tested than when a group of more widely varying abilities is investigated. If a single grade level is used in establishing the reliability of a test, for example, the coefficient undoubtedly will be smaller than if two or three grade levels are used. The reliability coefficient of a musical achievement test or of a musical aptitude measure will be smaller if derived from administration of the test to college music majors than to an unselected group of college students. Consequently, the reliability coefficient given in any test manual or cited in any literature concerning testing should be viewed in the light of the variability of the group with which the coefficient was derived. Some measure of the variability of the group, preferably the standard deviation, should be included in the covering material.

Since interpretation of a reliability coefficient depends upon the variability of the test group, a different expression of reliability may be used to avoid this influence. This is the *standard error of measurement*. The standard error of measurement for a test can be derived by formula, using the reliability coefficient and the standard deviation of the sample group with which the reliability coefficient was derived. It is based on the concept that a testing is only one sample of a subject's behavior or ability in the area covered by the test and that, if other samples of this behavior were obtained, that subject's scores would vary within a given interval. Since it is a kind of standard error, the standard error of measurement estimates the size of the interval within which that variation would occur and the probabilities of its occurrence within that interval. If the obtained score on a test is 67, for example, and the standard error of measurement has been found to be 3, it can be assumed with two chances in three of being correct, that the subject's true score would lie between 64 and 70 —scores lying at one unit of standard error of measurement below and above the obtained score. This method of expressing reliability is independent of the variability of the sample group, and for that reason it is preferable to the reliability coefficient for some purposes. Since the standard error of measurement is expressed in terms of units of score on the test, however, it is not comparable from one test to another. It has not been used as frequently as the reliability coefficient in connection with music tests.

The reliability coefficient of a test can be influenced also by the general difficulty level of the test in relation to the general ability level of the group tested. Tests which generally are very easy for the trial group may tend to show higher reliability coefficients, but they may be poor measures in that they do not detect those subjects capable of making finer distinctions. A measure of pitch discrimination which requires the subject to hear no differences smaller than a semitone, for example, may very well produce more consistent results (and hence a higher reliability coefficient) than one which includes smaller differences in pitch. Since ability to hear differences in pitch much smaller than a semitone is important in many types of musical activity, however, such a test may not be of much practical value for guidance in music activity.

On the other hand, a test which includes too many items which require finer discriminations than the subjects are capable of will be unreliable. In such a case guessing will have a significant influence. This should be reflected, however, in the reliability coefficient of a measure of this nature.

A test chosen for use in any situation should be of a difficulty level appropriate for the group with which it is to be used. It should include items difficult enough to measure the ability of the highest aptitudes or of the greatest degree of accomplishment in the group, and it should also include, if possible, items easy enough for all to master. It is especially important that a test include a sufficient number of items at each level of difficulty to ensure reliable results.

It is apparent from the foregoing discussion that reliability coefficients must be interpreted with care in the light of other factors. For this reason test manuals and test literature should include sufficient information to permit intelligent evaluation of reliability estimates. Information essential for intelligent interpretation of reliability coefficients includes:

(1) The method by which the reliability coefficient was derived. If the retest method was used, the period of time which elapsed between testings should be reported. If a split-half technique was used, the basis of division of the test should be specified.

(2) A description of the group used in the derivation of the reliability coefficient. This description should include age or grade level, sex, general background, and as much additional information as possible concerning the characteristics of the group.

(3) Statistical information pertinent to interpretation of a reliability coefficient. This should include the number of cases used, the mean score, and especially a measure of variability—preferably the standard deviation.

(4) A description of the sampling method used. The report should specify how the sample group was selected. It should include, also, some estimate of the sampling error.

The reader inevitably will ask: "What is a satisfactory reliability coefficient?" There is no simple answer to this question. Not only are other factors significant in the evaluation of a reliability coefficient, as already indicated, but the purpose for which the test is to be used also must be considered. If a test is to be used for group measurement, i.e., to separate those subjects who have a fair chance of success from those with little chance, it need not have as high a reliability coefficient as it must to be satisfactory for individual measurement, i.e., to rank individuals within a group or to determine one person's respective levels in various abilities or attributes.

Kelley[4] suggested a table of values, arbitrarily derived, to assist the novice in evaluating reliability coefficients for several purposes. His suggestion is as follows:

a) To evaluate level of group accomplishment........................ .50
b) To evaluate differences in level of group accomplishment in two or more performances................................... .90
c) To evaluate level of individual accomplishment................ .94
d) To evaluate differences in level of individual accomplishment in two or more performances....................... .98

More recently Leonhard and House[5] have summarized opinions concerning useful degrees of reliability in the following table:

.85-.99   High to very high; of value for individual measurement and diagnosis

.80-.84   Fairly high; of some value in individual measurement and highly satisfactory for group measurement

.70-.79   Rather low; adequate for group measurement but of doubtful value in individual measurement

.50-.69   Low; inadequate for individual measurement but of some value in group measurement

Below .50   Very low; inadequate for use.

Under some circumstances use of a test with a reliability coefficient of less than .50 may be justified if it is the best measure available. If, for example, an organization wished to pick from a group those most likely to succeed in some special task or training and no measure with a reliability coefficient above .50 could be obtained, a measure with a lower coefficient would probably assist in improving upon simple subjective judgment. In any case, of course, the higher the coefficient the better, but any measure which offers improvement upon mere chance should not be summarily rejected.

---

[4]T. L. Kelley, *Interpretation of Educational Measurements.* Yonkers, N.Y.: World Book Co., 1927, pp. 28-29. Used by permission of the copyright owner.

[5]Charles Leonhard and Robert W. House, *Foundations and Principles of Music Education.* New York: McGraw-Hill Book Co., 1959. pp. 341-2. Reprinted by permission of the copyright owner.

While the foregoing tables may be of considerable help to those inexperienced in statistics and testing, it must be kept in mind that these are arbitrary generalizations. Evaluation of the reliability of any measure is a complex problem. Desirable as it might be, there is no quick and easy method.

In some literature the reader may find the reliability of a test expressed in an *index of reliability*. This index is the correlation between a set of obtained scores and their theoretically true counterparts. It is equal to the square root of the reliability coefficient. The reliability estimate of a test may appear to be higher, therefore, if expressed by an index of reliability than it will if expressed as a coefficient of reliability. For example, a reliability coefficient of .81 is the equivalent of an index of reliability of .90 since the index is equal to the square root of the reliability coefficient and $\sqrt{.81} = .90$.

A word of caution concerning the distinction between the reliability of the test itself and the reliability of the testing or administration of the test is, perhaps, in order at this point. In defining test reliability as the consistency of a test, one ignores for the moment any conditions outside the test itself which might affect the results attained and, consequently, the consistency of results. It is assumed that the test is given under conditions which permit each subject to produce results truly representative of his ability in that field. Reliability of the actual test administration, a very important consideration in the field of measurement, will be discussed in Chapter 5.

Validity

A satisfactory level of reliability is an important characteristic to seek in a test. It must be remembered, however, that a reliability coefficient provides an estimate only of the consistency with which the test measures. It gives no indication of whether or not the test measures what it purports to measure or what the user wishes to measure. The latter, obviously, is an extremely important quality to look for in a test.

The extent to which a test measures what it purports to measure is termed the *validity* of the test. Thus, a measure of musical aptitude should measure potential for some kind of achievement in music. A test of musical achievement should measure some kind of learning or accomplishment in music. Validity, in a sense, is the truthfulness of a test.

Although test validity commonly is defined as in the foregoing, i.e., the extent to which a test measures that which it purports to measure, a more practical definition might be "the extent to which a test measures that which is to be measured." A test is valid for a particular purpose, or it may be used for several different purposes and have a different degree of validity for each purpose. From a practical point of view it would seem to matter little if a test does not measure precisely what its title indicates if it is found to be a truthful measure of some other quality and is used for this purpose. A so-called intelligence test might be found, for example, to be a much more truthful measure of verbal comprehension than of more general intellectual aptitude. If the test is used to measure aptitude for verbal comprehension, then, it may be said that the test is valid for this purpose. Similarly, if a test is known to measure pitch discrimination it matters not, in a practical sense, if it is called a measure of musical talent or a test of musical aptitude. If one wishes to measure the ability of a subject or group of subjects to distinguish differences in pitch, such a test, provided that experience has shown it to be a true measure of pitch discrimination, is valid for that purpose. Whether or not pitch discrimination is a significant component of musical talent is another question and would have nothing to do with the validity of the pitch discrimination measure itself, as long as the test is used for that purpose only, i.e., to measure the extent to which the subject can distinguish differences in pitch. Admittedly, a test title should not be misleading, and a number of so-called "music talent" tests are vulnerable on this score. To fail to use a measure for the purpose for which it is valid merely because of a misleading title, however, seems less than good sense.

Content Validity. Three kinds of validity have been defined in the *Standards for Educational and Psychological Tests and Manuals* published by the American Psychological Association[6].

---

[6]American Psychological Association, *Standards for Educational and Psychological Tests and Manuals*. Washington, D.C.: American Psychological Association, 1966.

The first of these is "content validity," also referred to by some as "logical validity" or "curricular validity." Content validity is determined through analysis of test content and of the task or achievement to which the test allegedly is related. The test then is valid to the extent to which the material or content of the test represents a sample of the task or achievement which it is to measure. A classroom test in rudiments of music theory would rate high in content validity if analysis of test content revealed that the test items did indeed measure knowledge gained from instruction or study in this subject area. Content validity is pertinent primarily to achievement tests, whether standardized or teacher constructed, since this type of test is designed to measure attainment of a specific skill or of a specific body of knowledge or understanding.

Care must be taken in assessing logical validity that unwarranted assumptions are not made on the basis of the results of the test. If the test alluded to in the previous paragraph, for instance, tests the subject's knowledge of the staff, clefs, key signatures, etc., it can be said to be logically valid only as a measure of these *facts* of rudimentary music theory. To assume that a mere knowledge of key signatures, for example, indicated an understanding of the concept of tonality and that, consequently, this test were a logically valid measure of this somewhat more complex quality would be completely unwarranted.

Criterion-related Validity. This type of validity, known also as "empirical" or "statistical" validity, is essential to a test which is to be used to predict or estimate performance or standing in some pursuit or activity. It is determined by correlating scores on the test with some external criterion believed to give evidence of performance or standing. A test of musical aptitude might be used to predict chances of success in study of music, either in one particular music course or in a music curriculum. The criteria of success in the course or curriculum ordinarily would be grades earned, and the validity of the test as a predictor of success would be measured by the degree of correlation between test scores and grades in the music course or curriculum. Or the purpose of the test may be to predict chances of success in a musical career. Scores on the test then might be correlated with some other criterion of success, such as ratings of performance ability.

Criterion-related, or empirical, validity may be determined concurrently by correlating scores with existing criteria, or it may be predictive in that the validating data are gathered at some time after the testing. In the foregoing examples concurrent validity of the test might be determined by correlating scores with course grades or performance ratings existing at or before the time of the testing. Predictive validity would be established by giving the test to subjects whose progress in the course or in performance would then be evaluated at a later date.

In determining criterion-related validity, obviously, the validating criterion itself must be given careful scrutiny. Its own validity must be established before it can be used to determine the validity of a test. If course grades are used to validate a test of musical aptitude, the influence of other factors obviously not related to musical aptitude must not be overlooked. What is the content of the course? On what bases are course grades determined? In short, how valid are the grades? These are among the questions to be asked.

Subjective ratings offer no more certain means of validating tests, although in some cases they may provide the only practicable means. Subjective ratings are notoriously unreliable. Indeed, the demonstrated unreliability of subjective grading added great impetus to the move toward objective measurement. The competency of the person or persons supplying the estimates also inevitably affects the validity of this type of criterion. When subjective ratings are used as a validating criterion, therefore, it should be ensured that a sufficient number of ratings be obtained from well qualified persons. The greater the number of qualified ratings used, the higher the reliability of these ratings is likely to be. The validity of such ratings, of course, is in direct proportion to the competence of the individuals rendering them.

Construct Validity. The third kind of validity is known as *construct validity*. A construct may be defined as a hypothetical trait conceived or *constructed* in the mind of an investigator to account for regularities in behavior. For example, a musical person may be expected to behave differently, at least in interaction with musical phenomena, than an unmusical one. Musicality, then, might be considered a construct which accounts for certain regularities of behavior of those persons thought to be musical. Construct validity of a test refers to the degree to which the test scores are consistent with judgments resulting from observing behavior believed to be related to the psychological theory or construct with which the test is associated. If persons scoring high on a test of musicality, therefore, manifest behavior held to be the result of the construct *musicality* and those failing to manifest such behavior score low on the test, the test may be said to have construct validity.

Construct validity of a new test sometimes can be determined by correlating it with an existing test which already has been found to be a valid measure of the construct under investigation. Intercorrelations of the test with several others may identify one or more common factors measured by all the tests and thus establish *factorial validity*, a type of construct validity. Factorial validity, however, is of little value unless there is some other satisfactory evidence of relationship between the common factors and the construct in question.

Construct validity is of particular importance with tests of psychological traits when the test user wishes to increase his understanding of the traits which the test measures.

A given test may well possess more than one of these kinds of validity. The validity of a test is related to the purpose for which it is used, and the same test may be used for different purposes at different times. Careful analysis of a test used to measure achievement in a music course or in a group of courses, for example, should indicate that it is a representative sample of the content of the course or courses; i.e., it should possess content validity. In the belief that past achievement is a good predictor of future achievement in a similar but more advanced course, the same test might be used to predict success in the more advanced course. Its value for this purpose would depend upon its criterion-related validity, determined by correlating test scores with course grades.

In addition to these three kinds of validity, there is a type of pseudo validity which should be mentioned. "Face" validity may sometimes be confused with logical or content validity. Face validity refers to the *apparent* truthfulness of a test. Does it appear to measure what it is used to measure? Does it seem to be relevant to its objectives?

Face validity, obviously, is not true validity. It is, however, of some indirect significance. A test should appear to those who take it to be relevant or appropriate to its purpose. The result otherwise may be poor cooperation, no matter how high the objective validity of the test. Some music tests have been criticized on this basis because they use sound stimuli which are unmusical. Face validity, however, should never be accepted as a substitute for objectively determined validity. While the two may be combined in a test, they are unrelated, and the presence of one is not evidence of the presence of the other.

As may be inferred from the foregoing discussion, reliability is a prerequisite for validity of both tests and validating criteria. If a test is not reliable, it cannot be valid. A test can be reliable without being valid, however. Repetition of a falsehood does nothing to diminish its falseness, and a test may produce very consistent results without measuring the trait under investigation. While it may then be valid for some other purpose, it cannot be said to be a valid measure of this particular trait.

Again the question inevitably arises, "What is a satisfactory validity coefficient?" This question is more difficult to answer in general terms than the similar query posed with reference to reliability. Validity coefficients of different types of tests differ markedly from one another, and some methods of validation produce generally higher coefficients than others. Correlations between group intelligence tests and established objective criteria, such as the Stanford-Binet test, frequently have ranged in the eighties. When criteria of a more subjective nature, such as course grades or ratings, have been used, however, the coefficients customarily have been somewhat lower. Validity coefficients for vocational aptitude tests, which frequently are derived from correlations with ratings of job performance, seldom have risen above .60 and most are well below this level. Industrial counselors often use aptitude tests with validity coefficients well below .50 in screening job applicants.

In evaluating a validity coefficient, then, it is necessary to consider the general level of such coefficients for that type of test or for the type of purpose for which the test is to be used. Validity coefficients in the .40's and .50's usually have some significance for musical aptitude measures, especially when course grades or ratings have been used as the validating criterion. In many such cases, the validity coefficient has been derived with a relatively small and often highly select group—factors which tend to reduce coefficients.

In general, any positive correlation probably indicates that decisions based on the information provided by the test probably will be more sound than those made without data. Whether or not a test with a low validity coefficient is worth using depends upon several factors, including the urgency of the need for data, the cost involved, etc.

Since a validity coefficient is a coefficient of correlation, it is influenced by the same factors which must be considered in evaluating correlation coefficients in general. In evaluating any validity coefficient, then, one must keep in mind the variability of the group used in deriving the coefficient, the number of cases used in the study, the purpose for which the test is to be used, and the reliability of the test and of the validating criterion.

Miscellaneous Practical Aspects

In addition to the technical qualities of reliability and validity a number of other characteristics must be considered in evaluating a test for use in any situation. Many of these might be grouped conveniently under the heading of *practicability*. While practicability cannot substitute for validity and reliability, a measure which is impracticable for any situation is valueless for that situation, no matter how sound technically.

One of the aspects of practicability, of course, is cost of the test. Tests which are unreasonably expensive will be avoided in many situations regardless of their technical excellence. False economy should be avoided, however, in selecting tests for use. A cheap test may prove more expensive than one with a higher price if the former is weak in validity and reliability. An invalid test is too expensive at any price. Similarly, the cost of a test always must be balanced against the possible cost of dispensing with the test, since the cost of buying and administering a test might possibly be returned many times over in improved guidance.

Fortunately, most published music tests are relatively inexpensive. In several measures of musical aptitude and in one or two of musical achievement the principal expense consists of the original purchase of phonograph records. If cared for, these can be used repeatedly for a considerable period of time. Replenishment of supplies of answer sheets, usually the only subsequent expense, also can be accomplished at relatively little cost. There are differences among prices of music tests, of course, but as with tests in other fields, price often is not a true indicator of value. The more expensive test is not always the more valid nor, therefore, the more desirable.

Ease of administration and scoring should be given significant weight in the selection of a measure for any situation. If a test can be administered only by specially trained personnel, or if it requires the use of elaborate and costly technical equipment, it may be impracticable for many schools. Fortunately, most music tests rate fairly well in this respect. The published tests, both of aptitude and of achievement, require no apparatus more complex or expensive than an adequate phonograph or tape player, and most of them require relatively little special training on the part of the test administrator.

Most published music tests now make use of an answer sheet which can be scored by machine. Stencils usually are provided also, so that small quantities of papers can be scored quite easily by hand. Scoring, therefore, presents no real problem with most of these measures.

The amount of time required for administration and scoring also affects the value of a measure. Not only is an unusually time consuming test often difficult to fit into the school schedule and costly in teacher time, but it may become boring or even antagonizing to the subjects to whom it is administered. Antagonism on the part of the subject can make useless the administration of any measure.

Clarity and completeness of instructions are further important considerations in administering a test and in evaluating results according to the established norms. Incomplete or unclear instructions to the subject weaken the standardization of a measure and increase the difficulty of accurate evaluation of results. Instructions, therefore, should be couched in language appropriate to the age level for which the measure is intended. As a further aid to understanding on the part of the subjects, opportunity for trial attempts should be given. Some recorded measures of musical aptitude include the instructions on the record with the test items. This helps to ensure consistency of instructions in different situations and thus it contributes to standardization of procedures. It also reduces the opportunity for guided trials, however, and eliminates questions. Whether this disadvantage is sufficient to nullify the advantage of standardized instructions is open to question.

The manner in which test items are separated and organized also is of importance—perhaps especially so in tests involving auditory acuity. Precautions should be taken that the subjects do not lose their places. Young children, particularly, can easily become confused. Some music tests meet this need by numbering items aloud on the record, thus helping the subject to keep his place or to rediscover it if once lost. Other music tests, however, are vulnerable on this score.

In tests which utilize some kind of sound stimulus the type of stimulus used also is an important element in the measure. Certain test batteries have been criticized on the grounds that the sound stimulus used is unmusical, is boring or unpleasant to the subjects, or is objectionable for some other reason. Some measures have been revised, partly in acknowledgment of such objections. Others, appearing at later dates, have used new types of stimuli in the hope of overcoming the objections leveled at their predecessors.

The degree of control of the stimulus used is of extreme importance since, without complete control of the sound stimulus, standardization of test administration and, consequently, reliability are seriously affected. Some measures, in attempting to use a sound stimulus of a more musical nature and more pleasing to the ear, have sacrificed control of the stimulus to a serious degree.

The medium through which the sounds involved are produced at the time of testing also is of great importance since here again control, and consequently standardization, is at stake. Several of the available measures of musical aptitude have been recorded; others are administered from the piano. Where the recording is of good quality, the former medium is to be preferred since a test played at the piano may not be administered with absolute consistency, no matter how conscientious the tester. Any error in the playing of any test item, even though immediately corrected, casts doubt upon the reliability of the testing and makes questionable the comparison of results with the established norms.

It is extremely important in any test that all factors be rigidly controlled so that results attained can be attributed with certainty to the factor being measured. In a measure of pitch discrimination which calls for a comparison of two sounds, for example, it is of extreme importance that the two sounds to be compared differ in pitch only. If any other factor such as loudness, duration, timbre, etc., is different, the subject's answer cannot be definitely attributed to the difference in pitch. Consequently, the validity of the results would be in serious doubt. This may be especially true when an answer of "same" or "different" is required.

A reliable table of norms is an essential part of any test manual. Sufficient information concerning the establishment of the norms should be given to ensure that valid comparisons can be made. The test manual also should provide the user with adequate information concerning the construction of the test, types of stimuli used and means of control of the stimuli, standardization procedures, etc. If all of this information cannot be included in the manual itself, the latter should at least provide references to accessible literature where such information can be found. Reliability and validity coefficients, together with an explanation of how they were obtained, must be available for any recognized measure. Failure of the author to provide such information, or to indicate readily accessible sources where it may be found, seriously detracts from the value of the test.

It is unfortunate that none of the currently available measures of either musical aptitude or musical achievement rate as high on all of these points as might be desired. Each has its own weaknesses as well as its strengths. It should not be assumed, however, that all factors are of equal importance in evaluating a test.

Although cost, motivation, ease of administration and scoring, etc., should influence the choice of a test for any situation, validity and reliability are absolute essentials of any measure. These must not be sacrificed for any other consideration if the measure is to be of value. In addition, since reliability and validity are dependent upon the scientific basis and control of the test, no measure which is weak in these factors is to be recommended.

Sources of Information About Standardized Music Tests

Readers can obtain information about standardized tests in music, both those which now exist and those which may appear in the future, from a number of sources.

Probably the best general source among these is the series of *Mental Measurements Yearbooks*[7] edited by Oscar K. Buros. These books, which have appeared periodically, include reviews of published tests in all fields and of books pertinent to tests and measurement.

Among the other sources are the *Journal of Research in Music Education, Journal of Educational Research, Review of Educational Research, Educational and Psychological Measurements, American Journal of Psychology, Journal of Educational Psychology, Journal of Applied Psychology, Journal of Musicology, Psychological Monographs,* and the *Bulletins of the Council for Research in Music Education.* Suggestions concerning the types of information relevant to reliability and validity which should be given in test manuals may be found in *Standards for Educational and Psychological Tests and Manuals.*[8]

SUMMARY

A number of characteristics are of great importance in the evaluation of any measure. Absolute essentials are reliability and validity. Since these depend heavily upon sound scientific pro-

---

[7]Oscar K. Buros (ed.), *Second, Third, Fourth, Fifth,* and *Sixth Mental Measurements Yearbooks.* Highland Park, N. J.: Gryphon Press, 1941, 1949, 1953, 1959, and 1964, respectively.

[8]American Psychological Association.

cedures in test construction, a sound scientific basis is an important asset to a test.

Other factors such as cost, ease of administration and scoring, time consumption, type of stimulus and medium, equipment and personnel required, clarity and completeness of instructions, and control of variables, also should influence the choice of a measure in any situation. Adequate information concerning the construction of the test, standardization procedures, and especially the establishment of reliability and validity should be available, and a satisfactory table of norms should be included in the test manual.

Although many factors are important, it must be remembered that no measure weak in reliability or validity is of much value no matter how satisfactory in other respects.

Questions for Consideration and Discussion

1. Distinguish between reliability of a test and validity of a test. Are these two test characteristics mutually dependent? Mutually independent? Explain.
2. What items of information should a test manual or description include as an aid to evaluation of a reliability coefficient? As an aid to evaluation of a validity coefficient? Why?
3. The validity of a musical aptitude test is investigated by comparing scores attained on it with grades attained by the same subjects in a course in music theory. What questions might be asked concerning the results of this study?
4. The same test of musical aptitude is investigated by comparing scores attained on it with ratings of performing ability given the same persons by a group of audition judges. What questions might be asked in this case?
5. What are the practical aspects to consider in evaluating a test for use? To what extent may practical excellence compensate for low validity in a test? For low reliability?
6. Is use of a test with a validity coefficient of less than .50 ever justified? If so, under what circumstances and why?
7. In comparing two tests, it is discovered that Test A has a reliability coefficient of .85 and a standard deviation of .06.

Test B also has a reliability coefficient of .85, but a standard deviation of .11. The trial groups used for establishing the coefficients were equal in size. Is there any difference in reliability between these two tests? Explain.

8. Which would be the more meaningful expression of reliability in each of the following cases:

   a) If one wishes to compare the reliability of two different tests of the same attribute?

   b) If one wishes to predict the general distribution of scores on a second administration of a measure already taken once by a group of subjects?

9. Which indicates a higher degree of reliability — an index of reliability equal to .85 or a coefficient of reliability equal to .81?

10. Distinguish among the "content," "criterion-related," "construct," and "face" concepts of validity. Give an example of each.

Recommended Readings

Anastasi, Anne. *Psychological Testing*. 3rd ed. New York: Macmillan, 1968. Chapters 4 and 5.

Cronbach, Lee J. *Essentials of Psychological Testing*. 3rd ed. New York: Harper and Bros., 1970. Chapters 5 and 6.

Garrett, Henry E. *Statistics in Psychology and Education*. 5th ed. New York: Longmans, Green, and Co., 1958. Chapter 13.

Guilford, J. P. *Psychometric Methods*, 2nd ed. New York: McGraw-Hill Book Co., Inc., 1954. Chapter 13.

Lindquist, E. F. (ed.) *Educational Measurement*. Washington, D. C.: American Council on Education, 1951. Chapters 15 and 16.

Stanley, Julian C. *Measurement in Today's Schools*. 4th ed. New York: Prentice-Hall, 1964. Chapter 5.

The Testing Situation

The reliability of measuring instruments was discussed in Chapter 4. In that chapter reference was made to a separate factor—the reliability of the testing, i.e., the administration of the test on a particular occasion. No matter how reliable and valid the measure itself, if the application of the measure does not result in a typical performance on the part of the subjects tested, the results are of little value. Several elements in the testing situation may have a significant influence on the reliability of the testing.

The Test Administrator

First, the tester himself. Who should administer measures of musical aptitude or of musical achievement? What are the characteristics of a good tester, and what principles must he observe?

It was pointed out in Chapter 4 that tests requiring lengthy special training for the tester probably are not practicable for many public school situations. Such a requirement would lessen the value of a test for many situations. In general, the administration of group tests requires less training on the part of the tester than does that of individual tests. Fortunately, this is true of most available measures of musical aptitude and of musical achievement.

Preparation for Testing. Certainly the person administering the test should be familiar with the test and with all instruments and equipment used in the administration of the measure. He should familiarize himself thoroughly with the instructions and procedures given in the manual and with the general form and content of the test. Materials such as test booklets, answer blanks, etc., should be checked and counted in preparation for the test administration. Instructions should be checked to ascertain if a special kind of pencil is needed and, if so, the test administrator should be sure that a sufficient number of suitable pencils is available. If tests are to be scored by hand it will be wise to provide pencils with fairly soft lead. The heavy marks made by such pencils will be appreciated during the scoring procedure.

If a phonograph or a tape player is involved, the tester should familiarize himself in advance with both the records or tape and the particular machine to be used. All machines do not operate in exactly the same way, and the test administrator must be completely sure of what he is doing and of what he must do next. Any mistake, or even hesitation, can seriously compromise the results of the testing. Even greater care is necessary, perhaps, if a piano is to be used. Although test items are usually elementary in their pianistic technical requirements, the player must be completely sure of himself. The elementary nature of the items is in itself a cause for greater caution on the part of the player, since it can lead to overconfidence. Any carelessness which results in a momentary slip or hesitation again compromises the test scores. No correction or admonition to the subjects to ignore the incorrectly played item can rectify the error once it has been made. The propensity for such slips, even when the pianist is highly experienced, casts doubt upon the desirability of the piano as a means of administering music tests. In the interests of accuracy and standardization, some form of recording is preferable as the medium of presentation.

In certain circumstances it may be desirable to divide the duties of administering a test between two persons, one to give instructions, etc., and the other to play any musical items included, whether at the piano or the phonograph or tape player. In this way each can devote his entire attention to one aspect of the test procedure.

Giving Instructions. Although the administration of most group tests is not a difficult accomplishment, there are several principles which the tester must observe if a reliable testing, which can be compared with established norms, is to result. The directions given in the test manual should be followed closely. *Instructions to the subjects should be given exactly as found in the test manual.* Any paraphrasing or supplementation of the standard instructions may make invalid the comparison of scores with the established norms. Opportunity is provided the subjects, of course, for asking questions, and the test administrator should do his best to make sure that each subject understands clearly what he is to do. It is not always easy to answer such questions without providing the subjects with supplementary information which weakens the standard nature of the testing, but the tester must make every effort to avoid giving significant additional information in answering questions.

In giving instructions the tester should read them slowly and distinctly, making sure before he starts that he has the attention of all subjects so that repetition will not be necessary. Instructions should be given singly, and each should be complied with before the next is given. Complex instructions should be avoided. It is best, whenever possible, to demonstrate the actions asked of the subjects, no matter how simple the instructions may appear. If, for example, the subjects are asked to turn to page 2 of the test answer sheet and to write their names in the upper right hand corner, these two actions should be separated. Holding up a sample and turning the page where all can see, the tester should instruct the subjects to turn to page 2 of the answer sheet. Then, after allowing a moment for the subjects to comply, he should point to the space provided and instruct them to write in their names. If the group is large the tester should have the assistance of a number of proctors who can circulate through the room to see that subjects do not fall behind because they do not understand.

The Tester's Manner. The tester's manner is important in the testing situation. It must be such as to put the subjects at ease while motivating them to give their best efforts. The tester should be absolutely impartial, but his manner should be neither coldly indifferent nor excessively authoritarian. A poised, pleasant manner, which treats the subjects as human beings rather than as cold statistics while maintaining the scientific impartiality essential to a good testing situation, is highly desirable in a test administrator.

It is important that the tester establish good rapport with the subjects with whom he is to work. Resentful or resistant subjects rarely will attain reliable results. A brief explanation of the purposes of the test and of its meaning to the subjects frequently is helpful in developing a cooperative attitude. Much depends, of course, on the age level of the subjects, the type of test involved, and other general aspects of the testing situation.

The test administrator should be watchful, too, for subjects who appear to be working under some temporary handicap. In group testing it frequently happens that one or more individuals in the group may be suffering from some minor disability. Colds, headaches, excessive fatigue and the like can cause unreliable results on the part of some individuals. Any such cases should be noted and, if possible, retested at some better time. The assistance of proctors in the test room is a great aid in detecting subjects who are working under unusual handicaps. Because some such cases may not be detected, however, it always is wise to regard low scores as tentative and to retest those subjects about whom there may be doubt.

Physical Facilities

The physical facilities used in the testing situation may have great influence upon the reliability of a test administration. The room should be adequately lighted and ventilated, and it should be large enough to permit proper spacing. It should be located so as to minimize distracting noises. This is especially important with tests involving hearing. Any noise which may conflict with a dictated test item or which may distract the subject's attention momentarily may have a serious influence on the test score.

Precautions should be taken that interruptions do not occur. It often is wise to place notices on the doors of testing rooms, indicating that tests are in progress and warning against intrusion.

Adequate writing space for each subject also should be provided. Inconvenient writing conditions may make it difficult for a subject to keep up with a test, or to proceed at a rate which would produce the best results. The subject's attitude may be affected, also, if he is required to work under adverse conditions at a time which is important to him. Adequate room facilities are a help, too, in controlling cheating. This is a distasteful subject to most teachers and test administrators, but its influence upon test results cannot be ignored. Good spacing of test subjects is one of the most effective methods of eliminating copying in the test room. Again, the assistance of an adequate number of proctors also is a great aid.

Equipment

Any equipment used in administering a test should be adequate for the purpose. This means that it should be of satisfactory quality and that it be in good operating condition. Most measures of musical aptitude are recorded and, therefore, require a phonograph or tape player. Any phonograph used must be of high quality, with a turntable which revolves steadily and accurately at the correct speed. Any unsteadiness in the turntable will result in distortions in pitch and loudness of the test items presented, and this seriously affects the testing. The instrument must have power sufficient to produce all items with sufficient volume without distortion, and it should be free from amplifier hum and any other extraneous sound which might interfere with the production of the test items or which might distract the subject's attention. It is obvious that small portable phonographs, unless of unusual quality, are not suitable for such work. Records should be free of scratches and excessive surface noise, and the tone control on the phonograph should be set at the proper level. Use of an inappropriate playback curve may distort the sound sufficiently to affect the test results. Some music tests now are available on tape. The tape recorder machine offers several advantages over disc records, and it is to be hoped that more tests will be recorded in this way. Care still must be taken, of course, to ensure that both tape and player are capable of faithful reproduction.

If a piano is to be used for administration of a test, it should be well in tune and free from any extraneous noises or vibrations. The key mechanism should be in good working order so that test items can be played accurately. A sticky key can distort a rhythmic pattern easily.

Although a few test manuals speak of administering the measure to groups of two or three hundred simultaneously, it usually is advisable to divide such groups into much smaller sections. Phonograph equipment of even the highest quality will not function satisfactorily in too large a room, and if a piano is used, the large group is at an even greater disadvantage.

The Testing Period

It is inadvisable, also, to attempt too long a testing at one sitting. With hearing tests, in particular, fatigue may become influential within a relatively short time. This may vary slightly according to the type of sound stimulus used. Test batteries consisting of several separate measures are best administered in several sittings, the number depending upon the number of measures in the battery, the age of the subjects involved, and other factors in the testing situation.

Scoring

Care is necessary, too, in the scoring of tests. Several methods of scoring tests are in common use. The choice among them usually depends upon the type of answer procedure involved and the number of papers to be scored.

Many tests now are provided with answer blanks which can be scored either by machine or by hand with the aid of a cut-out stencil. Such tests consist of multiple choice items, and the subject fills in the space between two parallel lines which stand beside or beneath the answer of his choice. If the papers are to be scored by machine, special soft pencils must be used and the subjects should be admonished to record their answers with heavy marks.

They also should be cautioned against making any marks except in the spaces provided for the answers of their choice. Correct answers which are not marked heavily enough may be missed by the machine, and extra marks may be scored as incorrect answers.

Machine scoring is the preferred method when there are large numbers of papers. When smaller numbers are involved, these blanks can be scored by hand with the aid of a stencil. The stencil consists of a sheet of heavy paper, plastic, or light cardboard with holes punched in appropriate positions. When this sheet is placed in the proper position over an answer blank, the holes reveal the correct answers. The scorer then can go quickly over the paper, making some kind of mark on each correct answer which the stencil reveals. It is wise, when using such a stencil, to check each answer blank to see that only one space has been filled in for each answer. The stencil exposes only one space—the correct answer—for each item. Conceivably, by filling in all spaces for an item, the test subject could ensure a correct answer if the scorer is careless and does not check for multiple answers. A quick check of the answer blank before putting the stencil in place will reveal multiple answers. It then is helpful to draw a line through the entire item in which this occurs, so that the line will appear through the stencil cut-out. The scorer must take care, also, that he has the proper stencil and that it is correctly placed over the answer sheet.

Another type of stencil has been used with answer blanks which require the subject to write in a number or a letter for each item. In such a case a set of stencils, equal in number to the number of choices which the subject has, is used. Each stencil is cut so as to reveal the positions of certain letters or numbers. For example, if the subject is required to answer S (same) or D (different) to the items included, two stencils will be used. One is cut so as to reveal the spaces which would be filled correctly with S's. If a D is revealed by this stencil, that answer, of course, is incorrect. The other stencil reveals the spaces which should be filled with D's, and any S's exposed are marked incorrect. Since this method is more cumbersome than that previously described, and especially since many test authorities prefer answer forms which do not require the subject to write in a word or letter, some measures which used this latter type of answer in early versions have in later editions turned to the other type of answer and blank.

A scoring device commonly used for measures which require the subject to write in a response is the folded key sheet which reveals only one column of answers at a time. By folding the sheet so as to expose only the appropriate column of answers, the scorer can place the key answers directly beside the answers on the test blank. This procedure eliminates much head and eye movement. Although this device facilitates the scoring of answers of the written-in type, it is quite cumbersome in comparison with any of those already described.

SUMMARY

The testing situation is a factor which can have great influence upon test scores. The competence and manner of the tester, the preparation of materials and equipment, and the quality and condition of equipment and room facilities are among the important elements in the testing situation. In tests involving hearing some type of recorded presentation of test items is preferable to administration from the piano, since the former ensures greater accuracy and greater consistency of performance in different administrations of the test.

Several methods of scoring tests are available. The choice of method usually is determined by the type of answer required and by the number of papers to be scored. Machines, stencils, and folded key sheets are among the methods most frequently used.

QUESTIONS FOR DISCUSSION

1. How is the reliability of the testing situation different from the reliability of a test? What is the relation between the two?
2. How should one prepare himself for the administration of a standardized test? What other preparations should he make?
3. In giving instructions for a test, what precautions should be observed?
4. Think of your own experiences as a test subject. Can you describe the manner of the test administrator on any occasion? What were your reactions to him in the situation? How might his manner have affected test results?

5. Consider the room in which you find yourself at this time. Would it be suitable for administration of a musical aptitude test? If so, would there be any limitations on its suitability, i.e., would it be suitable for certain types of test but not for others? How else might it be limited? If the room is not suitable at all, why isn't it?
6. Consider the phonograph available for use by your class. Is it suitable for use in the administration of a recorded musical aptitude test? If so, would there be any limitations on its use for this purpose?
7. What precautions should be taken in scoring tests?

RECOMMENDED READINGS

Anastasi, Anne. *Psychological Testing.* 3rd ed. New York: Macmillan, 1968. Chapter 2.

Cronbach, Lee J. *Essentials of Psychological Testing.* 3rd ed. New York: Harper and Bros., 1970. Chapters 3 and 4.

CHAPTER **6**

Psychological Bases
of Musical
Aptitude Tests

The value of any measure of musical aptitude is directly dependent upon the psychological assumptions upon which it is based. Measures based upon invalid theories of musicality hardly can provide valid appraisals of capacity for musical achievement. For this reason a brief review of the outstanding theories concerning the nature of musicality seems in order, even though this volume is concerned only with measurement and evaluation in music rather than with the psychology of music in general.

Musical Aptitude, Musical Talent, Musicality, and Musical Ability Defined

In psychological literature some confusion surrounds the use of the terms musical aptitude, musical talent, musicality, and musical ability. These have not been used consistently by different writers. While it seems unnecessary to examine these specific differences at this time, definition of these terms for the present context undoubtedly will help to avoid further confusion in this discussion.

The distinction between these terms which will be observed here may be somewhat simpler than that made by some writers. Musical aptitude is used in the present context in the sense of potential or capacity for musical achievement—those qualities or traits which permit or facilitate the acquisition or development of musical skills. Musical talent and musicality also are used in this sense. All three imply the potential for achievement in musical learning, but are not themselves necessarily affected by such learning. Musical ability, on the other hand, refers to musical powers, whether native or acquired. Musical ability can be demonstrated by performance or composition, or by some other response in a musical situation. Thus, we may speak of one's ability to play the piano, or to sing, etc. In doing so we refer to how well that person can play the piano or sing at that time, without concerning ourselves with the question of whether that person's proficiency is attributable mainly to natural endowment or to learning.

The Study of Musicality

The general approach to the description of musicality has been through analyses of musical ability in an attempt to identify those traits responsible for musical behavior. Such analyses have come from general observations on the part of psychologists and music educators, and from detailed studies of persons known to be musical.

The interest of psychologists in the nature of musical talent is recorded in documents coming from the late years of the nineteenth century. Among the first to suggest some criteria of musicality were Billroth[1] and Stumpf.[2] Further studies were made during the first two decades of the twentieth century.

A number of the investigations into the nature of musicality have taken the form of analyses of the personalities of acknowledged musical persons. Additional knowledge has been gained from studies concerned with the inheritance of musical talent.

---

[1]v. Max Schoen, *Psychology of Music*. New York: The Ronald Press Co., 1940. p. 152.
[2]Loc. cit.

Studies of these two types resulted in inventories of traits found to be prominent in musical persons and presumed, therefore, to be largely responsible for their musical behavior.

Attributes of Musicality. The inventories compiled by different investigators were by no means identical. Opinions differed as to the number of attributes significant in musical ability, and especially as to the relative importance of certain traits. Although differences between methods of investigation undoubtedly contributed to the variance of findings, the lack of unanimity emphasizes the complex nature of musicality.

A number of attributes, however, appeared in several such inventories. Prominent among these common traits were the ability to detect small differences in pitch, the power to retain and recognize melodies or chords, absolute pitch, the ability to distinguish between intervals of different sizes, rhythmic sensitivity, the ability to analyze out the constituents of chords, and some discrimination of purity of intervals or of degrees of consonance.

An examination of the measures of musical aptitude devised by various psychologists and educators in the twentieth century makes evident the influence that these studies have had upon attempts to appraise musical talent. While none of the measures includes all of these common traits, each test or test battery does include several of them. Of this list, only absolute pitch is ignored by all of the measures. This omission may well be due to the extreme difficulty of measuring this attribute. It also may be due to recognition of the fact that, while many fine musicians do possess this ability, many more of at least satisfactory accomplishments do not.

Theories of Musicality

Theories of the nature of musicality and of its measurement seem to have developed in general along two divergent and fairly well defined lines. One school of thought views musicality as a complex of a number of separate and relatively independent attributes. Psychologists of this school have attempted to identify these constituent traits and to isolate as many of them as possible for measurement.

Prominent among the proponents of this view was Carl E. Seashore, one of the most significant figures in the field of measurement in music. Seashore analyzed musicality into capacities for the hearing, the feeling, and the understanding of music.[3] He included also an interest in or an urge toward music, and he believed that ordinarily these would be supplemented by some capacity for the expression of music. Of these, the capacities for the hearing of music are basic to the others. Music must be heard before it can be understood and before any affective response to it can take place.

This belief obviously places great importance upon sensory capacities. Seashore was careful to point out, however, that musicality consists of far more than sensory capacity. He stressed the importance of musical feeling, imagery, and memory, and he insisted that these must be included in any appraisal of musical potential.

It was Seashore's further contention that, since music is conveyed from performer to listener by means of the sound wave, everything rendered and perceived as music can be expressed in terms of the physical attributes of the sound wave. Since the sound wave can be controlled at its source, it is possible to vary its properties under control. By varying certain properties of the sound wave in regulated degrees and noting the consequent responses of a listener it is possible, according to Seashore, to measure objectively and to express in specific terms the listener's ability to detect variations in the various aspects of tone, namely pitch, loudness, duration, and timbre.

Seashore imposed two conditions for scientific measurement: (1) the factor to be measured must be isolated so that effects can be attributed to specific causes, and (2) the conclusion must be limited to the factors under control.[4] In devising measures of musicality he restricted himself, therefore, to those among its constituent attributes which could be isolated and satisfactorily controlled. In so doing he admitted that the application of the

---

[3]Carl E. Seashore, *Psychology of Music*. New York: McGraw-Hill Book Co., 1939. p. 2.
[4]Ibid., p. 383.

measures would be limited, and he warned against attempts to derive any wholesale or generalized guide.

In Seashore's choice of pitch, loudness, duration, rhythm, timbre, and tonal memory as the elements of musicality to be measured there is no implication that these alone comprise the musical mind. He was most explicit in the expression of his belief that other factors such as imagery and thought are essential to the exploitation of sensory abilities. He did suggest that the mind can exploit only those elements of sound which are received and transmitted to it by the ear. To this extent, the more complex and subtle elements of musicality are dependent upon the sensory capacities.

Seashore believed, too, that the basic sensory capacities, namely the senses of pitch, loudness, time, and timbre are elemental, i.e., that they are functional at an early age and do not vary with training, intelligence, or increased age. The more complex forms of sensory capacity, the senses of rhythm, consonance, and volume (meaning size or magnitude), also are elemental, according to Seashore. Changes in the manifestation of these capacities, he held, should be attributed to clearer understanding or improved work habits in taking the tests, but not to any change in the capacities themselves.

A number of later studies of the possibility of improvement of certain of these attributes through training have raised serious doubts concerning their elemental nature. One such study frequently referred to was an investigation by Wyatt[5] of the improvability of pitch discrimination. This study led to the conclusion that, through intensive and carefully-planned training, this ability could be improved. Doubts of the elemental nature of these attributes, however, do not necessarily lead to rejection of the main part of Seashore's theory of the nature of musicality. This is not dependent upon the latter part.

Seashore referred to this theory that musicality can be analyzed into its constituent elements as the "theory of specifics." It has had a strong influence in the study of the psychology of musical

---

[5]Ruth F. Wyatt, "The Improvability of Pitch Discrimination." *Psychol. Monogr.*, 1945, 58:267, 1-58.

talent, and this influence has been reflected in the content and form of several measures of musical aptitude.

A number of psychologists and educators have rejected this theory of the nature of musicality and this approach to the measurement of musical aptitude. They have labeled the theory atomistic, insisting that musical talent is more than the simple sum of sensory and other identifiable capacities. They have sought a general factor responsible for musical behavior, and they have questioned the value of measures which are based upon the isolation of the simplest elements of musicality. These critics of the Seashore theory of the measurement of musical aptitude have called for tests of musicality which would measure this general factor, tests which present conditions more analogous to musical situations.

One of the most outspoken critics of the theory of specifics was James L. Mursell. Mursell supported a theory of musical talent generally consistent with the Gestalt approach to psychology. Adherents of this school of thought view things as wholes, believing that the whole is more than the simple sum of its parts. Mursell thus insisted that musical talent is more than a set of specific attributes dependent upon sensory capacities. He also emphasized, however, the complex nature of musicality or the musical personality, and he agreed with Seashore that different types of activity in music do not require all of the same abilities.

The most significant difference between the views of Seashore and Mursell and their respective adherents lies in the degree of importance which each places upon the sensory capacities. In Seashore's view the functioning of the musical mind depends directly upon its apprehension of those attributes of sound which are transmitted to it by the auditory sense. This obviously gives great importance to the sensory capacities.

Mursell, on the other hand, denied that sensory capacities are important ingredients of musicality.[6] To support this belief he cited a statistical study of the relative importance of psycho-

---

[6]James L. Mursell, *Psychology of Music*. New York: W. W. Norton Co., 1937. p. 323.

logical influences contributing to success in certain musical endeavors, a study which assigns a relatively small percentage of importance to the sensory capacities. One might question, however, the validity of this statistical type of basis for such a belief. In a statistical analysis of the various factors contributing to the satisfactory functioning of an automobile, a rather small percentage might well be attributed to fuel. Yet, without fuel, many of the other factors are rendered inoperative, and the machine will not function. Although the sensory capacities may represent but a small percentage of the many factors essential for successful musical endeavor of any kind, their importance may well be greater than their actual numerical weight.

Beliefs Concerning Validation of Aptitude Tests. Much of the controversy arising from these divergences between psychological beliefs has centered about the validation of musical aptitude measures. Seashore, consistent with his belief in the separate and independent nature of the capacities purportedly measured by the several tests in his *Measures of Musical Talents*, insisted that each test must be validated separately. He was emphatic that, since the measures dealt with only a small number of the factors involved in musical performance, no attempt should be made to validate any or all of them through comparison with any kind of over-all musical performance. Since the elements of musicality are not interrelated, it is useless, in Seashore's view, to attempt to validate a measure of any one of them through comparison with any type of musical activity which inevitably depends as well upon many other factors. Validity of the several measures can be estimated only through an appraisal of the internal consistency of each test as a means of determining whether or not the trait to be measured has been satisfactorily isolated and controlled. He was equally emphatic about any attempt to average or to combine the scores on the separate measures to provide a general or total aptitude score or ranking. Recognition of levels of capacity in the separate attributes, according to Seashore, is important in guidance since different attributes function in different degrees in various types of musical activity. Averaging or totaling of scores, therefore, would tend to thwart a principal purpose of the measures.

Mursell and others, however, held that a measure of musicality or musical aptitude should be validated empirically against some kind of musical activity. If the measure is valid, a person who attains a high score on the measure of musical aptitude thus can be expected to excel in performance, composition, or some kind of music study or activity. Conversely, those of high musical attainments will attain high scores on aptitude tests. Low attainments on tests and in musical activity should be similarly related. If a test could not be used for predicting success in some type of musical behavior, they insisted, it was not a valid measure of musical aptitude. Since the Seashore and similarly based measures failed in a number of studies to show a high correlation with success or lack of success in musical activity, it was held that they were not valid measures of musical aptitude, even though other investigations revealed high scores on these tests for a number of eminent musicians.

In fairness to the Seashore measures it should be pointed out, perhaps, that these studies were pursued with the original battery and that questions have been raised concerning the interpretations of certain results in some. More modern and more liberal views of standards for validity coefficients of aptitude tests would give at least some significance to some of those summarily dismissed as unsatisfactory in past years. Whereas validity coefficients of .50 and below generally were considered to be indicative of little value some years ago, further experience with aptitude tests and validating criteria has resulted in somewhat different expectations. Coefficients considerably below .50 are given some significance, at least under certain circumstances, and one reviewer of the Seashore measures has suggested that a validity coefficient of .40, when derived with a small select group, may be indicative of some value.[7]

Critics of the theory of specifics called for tests of musical aptitude which would measure talent in a more inclusive sense, and they insisted that these show significant correlation with success in musical activity. That great difficulties stand in the way of such

---

[7] Herbert Wing, in Oscar K. Buros (ed.), *Fourth Mental Measurements Yearbook.* Highland Park, N.J.: Gryphon Press, 1953. p. 344.

a measure is evidenced by the fact that no one has yet been completely successful in constructing a satisfactory test of this nature. Those measures of musical aptitude which have been put forth since the early Seashore battery also measure only certain factors believed to be important in musical accomplishment.

Authors of a number of later tests, however, have gone beyond the simple sensory capacities and have attempted to measure abilities in some of the more functional and more complex aspects of musical behavior. Kwalwasser and Dykema added to measures of sensory ability others designed to test certain types of imagery and taste. Gaston and Wing also have included measures of imagery and taste while ignoring the simple sensory capacities. Schoen, Madison, and Lundin, among others, have included some kind of interval discrimination, and the Wing battery asks the test subjects also to trace the movements of chord constituents in brief progressions. Most test authors have included some kind of measure of musical memory or retention.

This does not imply that all of the authors of these later tests deny the importance of sensory capacities. Several of them have attested to the essential nature for musical accomplishment of acuity in certain aspects of the auditory sense. Most of them, however, are in agreement in placing greater emphasis upon the functioning of sensory acuity in the perception of relationships among tones. Since very few independent studies have been made of the validity of any of these later tests, with the exception of the Kwalwasser-Dykema battery, there is not yet sufficient evidence available to support any definite conclusions concerning the validity of this more functional approach.

Most musicians and teachers would agree that certain abilities are essential for certain types of musical accomplishment. Few would disagree, for example, that the ability to distinguish small differences in pitch is an essential attribute for the person who would perform upon any instrument of variable pitch, including the voice. For, without this ability, the performer cannot possibly play or sing consistently in tune, and good intonation certainly is a prime requirement in musical performance. It is true, of course, that even with the ability to distinguish differences in pitch, the performer still may play or sing with poor intonation since other factors, such as motor control, play important roles in controlling intonation. But it is beyond question that, unable to hear small differences in pitch, the performer will not play or sing consistently in tune. Just how small a difference one must be able to distinguish is more difficult to determine. Certainly, however, any who hold that discrimination of differences smaller than the semitone is unnecessary since the latter is the smallest interval used in our system of temperament, take an untenable position. Most composers may not write relationships smaller than the semitone, but few would be satisfied if performers were no closer than a semitone to accurate pitch.

Other attributes also seem important to the musician, although some might not receive as general affirmation as pitch discrimination. Experienced music teachers are aware that at least some of these attributes vary independently. What teacher has not encountered the student with a "good ear" who experiences great difficulties with rhythms, or his opposite number who seems gifted with an acute perception of rhythm and ability to execute rhythms but who has difficulty in distinguishing differences in pitch.

It is evident that the foregoing statement with reference to ability to discriminate pitch differences pertains with equal validity to other sensory capacities. Possession of any sensory capacity in marked degree does not guarantee successful accomplishment even in endeavors depending heavily upon that particular trait. But deficiency in a sensory capacity probably forecasts lack of success in any type of musical activity which depends significantly upon that ability. Mursell admitted this with the following words:

> "Excellent and refined sensory capacity is in itself no guarantee of effective musical behavior. But extremely poor sensory capacity is a serious impediment to such behavior."[8]

Mursell's next words, perhaps, make the most important point concerning musical aptitude tests from the teacher's point of view. Speaking of the Seashore battery he continues:

> "Thus the tests reveal handicaps and disabilities rather than positive abilities. Here lies whatever utility they possess."[9]

---

[8]Mursell, op. cit., p. 324. Reprinted by permission of the copyright owner.
[9]Loc. cit. Reprinted by permission of the copyright owner.

It is difficult to imagine a musician or music teacher who would dispute the opening sentence of Mursell's statement. Even Seashore, the principal target of Mursell's criticisms, has never suggested the contrary.

Perhaps the most important difference between these prominent theories concerning the measurement of musical aptitude is in belief as to what elements of musicality can be measured satisfactorily. How complex an element can one measure without sacrificing adequate control of the medium and exactitude in the attribution of effects to causes? The answers of test authors to this question are reflected in the formats of their measures.

Utility of Aptitude Tests

It is the utility of musical aptitude tests which is of greatest importance to the music teacher. If it can be shown, therefore, that a particular test does measure with a satisfactory degree of validity a particular attribute generally believed significant for musical accomplishment, that test may be of practical use to the teacher in guiding students' endeavors and in diagnosing their difficulties, even though it cannot be accepted as a measure of musical potential in a positive sense.

The research studies which have raised doubt concerning the elemental nature of certain sensory capacities do not refute the utility of measures of these capacities. In few practical situations do teachers have either time or facilities to permit the kind of intensive specialized training used to effect improvement in sensory abilities in these research projects. Furthermore, where remedial procedures are feasible, valid measures can be of value in drawing to the teacher's attention those students in need of special help.

To be of even practical utility, of course, a test must be a valid measure of the attribute which it is used to measure. As a matter of practical utility, more concern can be given, perhaps, to the validity of a test as a measure of a single specific attribute than as a positive indication of a larger, infinitely more complex talent.

It is true that each such measure of specific attribute, no matter how valid in itself, can tell at best only a little about each subject measured. Those who hold that such measures are of value primarily in a negative sense undoubtedly are in the right. Any sensory capacity is but one link in a highly complex chain of abilities which contribute to successful control of only one aspect of musical performance. If one has the auditory acuity to hear small differences in pitch, he must have satisfactory control of the muscles necessary to the production of pitch, the intelligence necessary to learn how to develop such control, and the will to work at such development before he can learn to play or sing in tune. With all of these he can master only one among a great number of aspects of musical performance, yet one deficient link in the chain can render ineffective high levels in other abilities.

In conclusion it must be said that no more than tentative assumptions can be made at present concerning the respective merits of these different approaches to the measurement of musical aptitude. No sufficient body of evidence is yet available to confirm or refute either theory. Further research is needed either to confirm or refute the claims of test authors for the validity of their measures. Gauging of the more complex and functional elements of musical ability seems a highly desirable approach, and some of the efforts in this direction appear hopeful. The susceptibility of such elements to objective measurement, however, has yet to be proved conclusively. By the same token, the value of measures of specific attributes needs further investigation. It may yet be established that the two approaches aptly complement one another.

Summary

Psychologists in music have failed to reach agreement concerning the nature of musicality. Two schools of thought have been particularly prominent during the twentieth century: one placing heavy emphasis upon specific elements in musical ability and giving considerable importance to sensory capacities; the other viewing musical ability as a totality dependent upon a general factor and, consequently, considering sensory capacities somewhat less important.

Most of the musical aptitude measures which have been produced to date attempt to measure only certain aspects of musical ability. Some place heavy emphasis on sensory capacities, while others seek to measure more complex and, in the opinion of their authors, more functional elements of musicality. Most authors point out the importance of additional factors for musical accomplishment.

Further research is needed to establish the superiority of either approach. Since the early attempts to measure musical aptitude dealt principally with the most simple elements of musicality, more independent investigations have been made of the validity of this approach than of the other. Some of these investigations have supported the claims of validity of the measures; others have been cited as evidence that they are invalid. Some of the conclusions reached in some early studies might be questioned in view of more modern beliefs concerning validity coefficients of aptitude tests.

QUESTIONS FOR DISCUSSION

1. By what means have theories of the nature of musical aptitudes been developed?
2. Explain briefly the theory of specifics. What is the general factor theory of musical aptitude?
3. What are the basic differences in view concerning the measurement of musical aptitude? Which view seems best supported by the evidence at present?
4. What elements of musicality have various test authors attempted to measure?
5. What was Seashore's belief concerning the effect of training on the specific attributes measured by his *Measures of Musical Talents*? What evidence concerning this belief has been produced by later research? What effect does this evidence have upon the practical utility of the measures?
6. What conflicting views concerning the validation of musical aptitude tests have been prevalent?

RECOMMENDED READINGS

Farnsworth, Paul R. *The Social Psychology of Music*, 2nd ed. Ames, Iowa: The Iowa State University Press, 1969. Chapter 8.

Lundin, Robert W. *An Objective Psychology of Music*, 2nd ed. New York: The Ronald Press Co., 1967. Chapters 11 and 12.

Mursell, James L. *Psychology of Music*. New York: W. W. Norton Co., 1937. Chapters 9 and 10.

Schoen, Max. *Psychology of Music*. New York: The Ronald Press Co., 1940. Chapter 8.

Seashore, Carl E. *Psychology of Music*. New York: McGraw-Hill Book Co., 1939. Chapters 1 and 22.

CHAPTER 7

Problems in Music Testing

As in any field, objective measurement of achievement or aptitude for achievement in music confronts the test author with serious problems. Measurement of achievement and measurement of aptitude each presents its own problems and both share other difficulties which are inherent in the nature of music.

Aptitude Tests

In considering the problems of objectively measuring aptitude in music it is necessary, first, to arrive at an understanding of what is meant by "musical aptitude." To some the term means potential for achievement in some kind of musical performance or production, e.g., singing, playing an instrument, conducting, or composition. Others take a somewhat broader view, including as achievement in music the aural enjoyment and understanding of music. Although the latter is an important objective in music education and one toward the attainment of which objective measures may be of considerable help, potential for active accomplishment in performance has more often been the kind of aptitude which music teachers have been interested in measuring. Since performing and creative abilities in music demand those attributes necessary for intelligent listening and others besides, it may be considered the more complex type of aptitude. Any measure of aptitude for musical performance or production, therefore, may be assumed to measure also potential for musical enjoyment and understanding. The aptitude test author, consequently, may well proceed upon this assumption and work toward a measure of potential for musical performance or production.

Problems of Formulation. In developing a measure of aptitude, the test author is forced to observe several restrictions. Many of these are dictated by the purpose for which the test is designed. The prime purpose of an aptitude test usually is prognosis, although the measure often can be used for other ends as well. Aptitude tests in music, as in other fields, are needed for guidance. This means that they are used before training begins, or before it has progresed for long.

If an aptitude measure is to be used for prognosis, then, any items which require of the subject knowledge acquired through study or training must be avoided. No use can be made, consequently, of musical notation or terminology. In addition the test subject cannot be expected to make judgments based upon knowledge of conventions or principles of musical composition.

Several musical aptitude test batteries have included measures which do require knowledge of such aspects of music. Tests which require the subject to recognize in notation a melody which he hears, or which require him to perceive discrepancies between a pattern which he sees and one which he hears, obviously presuppose some knowledge of notation. Furthermore, even those who might still maintain that capacity for pitch discrimination is not improvable by training would agree that considerable practice is required for the coordination of eye and ear. This is attested by the intensive training in dictation and aural perception which is a part of all formal curricula of music study. Tests requiring knowledge and skill of these kinds may be of considerable value for certain purposes, but as prognostic measures they appear to be quite unsuitable, especially at the age levels where teachers might find the greatest need for prognostic tests.

Some other tests have attempted to measure taste or judgment. The subject may be asked to select the more appropriate of two endings for a melody, or to indicate whether a melody should terminate with ascending or descending movement. The place of tests of this type in an aptitude battery also may be questioned. What objective criterion can be applied in making such judgments? Only conformity to certain conventions or principles seems to fill the requirement of objectivity. This, obviously, requires knowledge of the conventions or principles involved, and the latter is at best a highly questionable criterion of aesthetic value. Musical taste of this type is almost certainly a matter of cultural conditioning. In the tests which attempt to measure this element, the "correct" answers are those which best conform to established principles of successive or simultaneous combination of tones—principles derived from the basic eighteenth-nineteenth century tonal style. To a child steeped in this melodic and harmonic idiom, the vocal polyphony of the Renaissance sounds strange, and the atonal styles of the twentieth century very likely are for him completely without meaning. Conceivably, then, a child whose musical taste is largely the result of exposure to commercial popular tunes, the banality of which is in large part due to stereotyped conformity to elementary eighteenth-nineteenth century principles of melodic and harmonic structure, might very well make a better score than one from a more highly cultured home environment in which he had been conditioned by a broader range of musical styles. Yet can it be said that the former has better aesthetic taste? The influence of such conditioning seems particularly incongruous in a measure which is to be used in an era which is witnessing the most significant changes in melodic and harmonic structures to have occurred in three centuries. Questions of this type might measure one's knowledge of certain styles of musical composition, but even as achievement measures they are limited in their application. What constitutes a correct answer in terms of the musical style of one period may be quite incorrect in terms of another.

The necessity for objectivity, then, raises doubts about measurement of certain aspects of musical ability. Aesthetic sensitivity certainly is an important factor in musical talent, but it is an element which has offered extreme difficulties in objective measurement. No really satisfactory method has yet been devised.

Other traits which have been suggested as significant elements of musical ability also have presented difficulties to the test author. Absolute pitch has appeared in several inventories of musical ability. It is a trait which can be measured only with extreme difficulty even in individual tests, and no way of group measurement seems practicable. This, therefore, is a trait which authors of group tests have ignored. It is, furthermore, a trait which probably would not show a high general correlation with musical accomplishment. Even though a number of investigators found this trait in several persons of marked musical ability, there is little doubt that many have accomplished much in music without it.

Ability to sing a melody also has been listed as an element in musical ability by several investigators. Here, too, is a trait which cannot be measured in group tests. Ability to sing or play a harmony part to a given melody, another symptom of musicality listed in certain inventories, is another attribute which is unapproachable through the group method.

Group tests are of necessity pencil and paper tests. Such tests, obviously, can include only items which can be answered by making some kind of mark on a paper. Any trait which can be manifested only through some active type of response, such as singing or playing, thus is not susceptible to measurement by group tests. Individual measurement of such abilities may be of great value in situations where time and facilities permit testing on an individual basis. In any situation individual tests may be recommended for checking of doubtful cases and for similar purposes, but the general need in most situations is for a valid group test.

It becomes apparent why authors of many group tests have attempted to measure only a few relatively specific elements of musical aptitude. Other elements either are not susceptible to objective measurement at all or do not permit the use of group testing techniques. In these circumstances, preparation of a satisfactory musical aptitude test of an omnibus type presents formidable problems.

Problems of Validation. The validation of musical aptitude measures presents problems as formidable as those involved in the devising of such tests. Since validity is the prime essential of any test, however, some method must be used to ensure that the test actually has a significant relationship to whatever it is used to measure.

Seashore insisted that internal consistency provided his *Measures of Musical Talents* with adequate validity. Each of the several tests in the battery was considered a valid measure of a specific element of musicality if item analysis showed that all items consistently dealt with that element. The validity of the traits measured as elements of musicality depends upon logical analysis of musical behavior as, then, does the validity of the entire battery.

In the light of the theory of specifics there seems to be considerable justification for this method of validation. If these capacities are independent and function differently in different types of musical activity, as Seashore and others have agreed, his insistence that attempts to validate any or all of them against over-all accomplishment in some kind of musical activity are unreasonable seems to have some logical basis. Too many other factors are influential in the complex of musical accomplishment.

Internal consistency, however, quite understandably, is for most persons inadequate as a validating criterion. To offer evidence that a test measures pitch discrimination or tonal memory is one thing. To demonstrate that pitch discrimination, or tonal memory, is an important factor in musical accomplishment is another. This can be established only through logical analysis of musical behavior, a means that is subject to question.

Some empirical method of establishing validity is highly desirable. That used most frequently with musical aptitude measures has consisted of comparison of test standings with ratings of talent or of accomplishment. Rating of accomplishment can be expressed directly or it can be formalized in grades earned in music study. Authors of many musical aptitude measures have presented such correlations as evidence of the validity of their measures and, even though Seashore expressly disapproved of the use of such methods with his *Measures of Musical Talents*, they have been subjected to far more independent studies of this type than have any other measures in the field.

Desirable as empirical validity is, ratings and grades are far from really satisfactory as validating criteria. Ratings are subjective and, consequently, as vulnerable to question as is logical substantiation of validity. In no area, probably, is this more true than in musical performance. Tastes differ. Musical performance is a complex of many elements, and there is no general agreement concerning their relative importance. Consequently, one listener may place great weight upon beauty of tone, while another places more importance upon accuracy. To another, that more intangible quality, sensitivity or expressiveness, may be more important than any of the others. In short, different persons place varying emphases upon different aspects of performance. There are few, if any, absolute standards of performance, and opinions differ even among well-qualified auditors. The influence of such variables can best be held to a minimum by averaging ratings from as many well-qualified judges as possible, but very often it is possible to obtain qualified ratings from only one or two. The value of any rating, of course, is in direct proportion to the qualifications of the judge who renders it.

Subjective ratings, too, are notoriously unreliable. While this can be detected in some instances, such checks on the consistency of ratings rarely have been applied in validation studies of musical aptitude tests. The question of reliability of ratings thus inevitably arises.

Course grades offer no significant advantages over less formal ratings. One might well ask first about the content of the course from which grades were used. Studies have been made comparing musical aptitude test scores and intelligence test scores with grades earned in certain courses. In several the conclusion has favored the intelligence test over the musical aptitude test as a predictor of course grades. Such a conclusion might well be anticipated if the course content is such that it emphasizes general learning rather than specifically musical accomplishment. In a course in History of Music, for example, one learns *facts* about the musical past in the same manner that he learns *facts* about social and political developments in more general history courses. Music appreciation courses of the past have been criticized upon frequent occasions because they so often emphasized facts about music rather than the music itself. In such cases one might very well expect grades to correlate more highly with general aptitude for learning than with capacities more peculiarly musical. Not all courses in History of

Music have the same emphases, nor do all music appreciation classes strive toward the same objectives. Knowledge of course content is essential, however, to the evaluation of any coefficient of correlation between course grades and aptitude test scores.

Even when course content is more peculiarly musical in nature, general aptitude for learning and other factors which function in all learning will strongly affect correlations between grades and test scores. A high level of musical aptitude may well be frustrated if general intelligence is substantially lower or if work habits conducive to accomplishment are lacking.

One might ask next about the bases upon which grades rest. How were they determined? Are they reliable? In many institutions, course grades may be affected by factors which have no direct relation to accomplishment, factors such as class attendance and punctuality of assignments. These, too, may influence the correlations.

The complexity of achievement in musical performance or in music courses is responsible for many weaknesses of ratings or grades as validating criteria. The influence of other factors inevitably lowers correlations between musical aptitude scores and ratings of musical accomplishment. This is especially true of measures of the more specific aptitudes.

Persons of known accomplishment certainly should exhibit these measurable traits in at least fairly high degree. High correlations could result, however, only if known failures in music revealed lack of such traits in significant degree. Too many factors other than these abilities may be the cause of failure to permit one to attribute it too easily to them. The contribution of other attributes such as aesthetic sensitivity, has been pointed out. Still other factors, not peculiar to musical achievement but certainly essential to it, further complicate the picture.

Intelligence has been mentioned with reference to course grades. This more general attribute, whether or not related to musical capacity, certainly is an important factor in all types of musical learning as in any other kind. Since much learning is required for accomplishment in musical performance or composition, failure in these fields quite obviously can result from deficiency in this more general aptitude for learning as well as from other causes.

In many types of musical activity, motor control is an important factor. Muscular coordination and dexterity of hands and fingers are essential for mastery of most musical instruments. An individual with high intelligence, acute sensory capacities, and fine aesthetic sensitivity may well be frustrated in musical aspirations due to an inability to develop satisfactory control of the essential muscles. Standardized tests of various types of motor ability have been devised, and some of these can supply information helpful to the music teacher. Most such tests, however, can be administered only on an individual basis.

For accomplishment in vocal music, there remains an important factor for which no hope of objective measurement seems to exist —the quality of the voice itself. This factor nonetheless will have a strong influence upon ratings of accomplishment. An individual with high general aptitude for music who has persisted in an unsuitable medium may well be rated a failure. His presence in a study, of course, would help to lower a coefficient of correlation even though an unfortunate choice of medium, rather than lack of general musical aptitude, would be the real cause of failure. Quite evidently we might expect to find musical attributes in satisfactory degree in some persons who have failed to achieve satisfactorily in musical endeavors.

Some investigators have sought to ascertain the validity of musical aptitude measures by correlating attainments on the measures with participation in certain types of musical activity. Thus, some have compared standings on musical aptitude tests of students active in certain types of musical organizations with standings on the same tests of students not active in such groups. Others have used continuance in music study as a validating criterion. While participation in musical organizations and continuance of music study probably are indicative of interest and interest may be indicative of aptitude, there are many who might question the latter. Furthermore, many other factors such as economic status, conflicting obligations or desires, and even personalities, have a strong influence upon participation and study. This fact weakens these as validating criteria.

Other investigators have turned to factor analysis as a means of validating musical aptitude measures. Factor analysis is an attempt to clarify the meaning of a test by studying its correlations with other variables. The investigator administers a number of tests to the same subjects in order to determine which of them measure the same traits and thus to reduce the number of traits necessary to the description of certain aspects of personality. Since such analysis depends upon the particular tests used, the results of the analysis are hardly more meaningful than the tests themselves. Under the circumstances, therefore, this method at present seems to offer no better evidence of validity than those already discussed.

Despite serious weaknesses, therefore, correlation of test rankings with ratings of performance or with course grades in music probably remains the most practicable method of investigating empirical validity of musical aptitude measures. The influence of other factors, however, must be kept in mind in evaluating coefficients derived by this method. It undoubtedly is an awareness of the difficulties involved in validation, gained from years of experience with aptitude tests, which has resulted in a liberalized view of validity coefficients. Coefficients which might generally have been considered insignificant three decades ago are now given some weight by testing authorities. In some circumstances, validity coefficients as low as .15 or .20 thus are considered indicative of some value. This may be true especially when the coefficients have been derived with relatively small, select groups—a frequent occurrence with measures of musical aptitude.

The array of difficulties, both in devising and in validating a musical aptitude measure, may appear discouraging to the reader. The limitations imposed upon musical aptitude measures by these difficulties may lead the teacher to dismiss the tests as inconsequential. It must be remembered, however, that every item of trustworthy information contributes to the total picture of the student. By piecing together reliable data obtained from various sources, the teacher may find himself far better equipped to guide his charges intelligently.

Achievement Tests

Since an achievement test is designed to measure mastery of a specific skill or body of knowledge, authors of music achievement tests have not faced quite the same problems as those who have sought to deal with aptitude for achievement.

Different authors have concerned themselves with different aspects of musical achievement. Many have dealt largely with knowledge of the rudimentary facts of musical notation, such as musical symbols and terms, although some also have included some attempt to measure the ability to associate the auditory and the visual by asking the subject to compare aural patterns with those given in notation on the test paper. Some have sought to measure knowledge of music history or literature or of facts of the musical world, such as names of composers and performers, while at least one has concerned himself exclusively with the auditory.

Several authors have devised measures of musical performance. Due to the nature of musical performance, these tests can be administered only on an individual basis. The value of such tests lies in the standardization of content, which permits comparability among different situations, and the attempt to systematize scoring.

Problems of Formulation. The principal problems involved in the formulation of a measure of musical achievement are the identification of the ability or knowledge to be measured and the construction of a good sampling of that knowledge or ability, thus ensuring content validity. Content validity of a test, of course, merely indicates that the test is a valid sample of the knowledge or skill which it is used to measure. It says nothing about the validity of the knowledge or skill itself as part of a curriculum or any other context. This must be judged in other ways.

Authors of measures of musical performance inevitably face the problem of objectivity. Certain aspects of performance, notably accuracy of rhythm and pitch, can be measured by relatively objective methods but other very important aspects of performance have not as yet yielded to objective measurement.

Achievement tests are used in some situations to predict chances of success in future study or activity. The Graduate Record Examinations and the National Teacher Examinations are examples of measures of achievement which customarily are used for predictive purposes, the former to predict chance of success in graduate study and the latter to estimate chance of success in teaching. This type of use is based on the belief, undoubtedly very sound, that past achievement is a good predictor of success at a more advanced level of the same study or pursuit. When used for such a purpose, however, an achievement test should demonstrate validity for this purpose, preferably through correlation of test scores with some kind of evidence of success in the advanced study or activity.

SUMMARY

The author of a measure of musical aptitude is faced with many difficulties and is hampered by many restrictions. Certain attributes believed to be important components of musical ability in general either are not susceptible to objective measurement or are unapproachable through group methods. Authors of group measures, consequently, have limited their tests to certain attributes or abilities which they believe can be measured objectively.

Validation of musical aptitude measures is complicated by the complexity of the various types of musical activity, the number and variety of factors involved in musical accomplishment, and by the lack of objective criteria of musical excellence. In these circumstances, high general correlations between musical aptitude test scores and ratings of musical accomplishment may be unattainable, regardless of the type of test involved. Current views evaluate validity coefficients of aptitude measures accordingly.

In the formulation of measures of musical achievement the principal problems are the identification of the knowledge or ability to be measured and the construction of a good sampling of that knowledge or ability. Authors of measures of musical performance face the difficulty of attaining objectivity since certain aspects of musical performance so far seem unapproachable through objective means.

QUESTIONS FOR DISCUSSION

1. Suggest some specific restrictions imposed upon the author of a group test of musical aptitude which need not concern the author of an individual test.

2. Suggest some factors which might cause discrepancies between ratings of one performance submitted by several different judges.
3. Why may low correlations between aptitude test scores and ratings of musical accomplishment present a misleading estimate of musical talent?
4. Suggest some irrelevant factors which might affect correlations between musical aptitude tests and grades in music theory; grades in applied music; grades in music appreciation.
5. What factors not peculiar to musical learning or accomplishment have a strong influence upon such learning or accomplishment?
6. Suggest the factors which may be especially important in each of the following areas of musical achievement: singing; piano performance; violin performance; snare drum performance; composition; conducting. Point out factors important in some of these but not in others.

Suggested Readings

For further information concerning factor analysis the reader is referred to:

Cronbach, Lee J. *Essentials of Psychological Testing.* 3rd ed. New York: Harper and Bros., 1970. Chapter 10.

Guilford, J. P. *Psychometric Methods.* New York: McGraw-Hill Book Co., 1936. Chapter XIV.

CHAPTER 8

Existing Musical
Aptitude Measures

Seashore. The earliest standardized battery of musical aptitude measures to appear in the United States was the Seashore *Measures of Musical Talent,* published in 1919. This battery included six tests designed to measure pitch discrimination, loudness discrimination, sensitivity to differences in time intervals, recognition of differences in rhythmic patterns, discrimination of degrees of consonance, and tonal memory. These measures attracted considerable attention, and they were subjected to investigation in a number of studies. Both approbation and strong criticism resulted.

Objections to the underlying theory of these measures and doubts of their validity have been discussed in earlier chapters. Other more specific objections were made to the various measures in the battery. In 1939 a revised edition of the Seashore Measures, the result of the work of Carl E. Seashore, Don Lewis, and Joseph G. Saetveit was published. Several changes had been made in an effort to eliminate weaknesses which investigations had revealed in the original battery. Many of the published discussions of the Seashore Measures, unfortunately, are based on the original version. While this is understandable, since many more studies were made of the original version than of the revised, such discussions do not always give the reader a true picture of the currently available Seashore battery. Since it is not always stated explicitly in publications which version is under discussion, the reader would be wise to check publication dates, not only of the publications themselves, but also of any studies cited. In this way he can arrive at a more valuable interpretation of such material.

The revised version of the Seashore *Measures of Musical Talents*[1] appeared in two forms. According to the test manual Series A was designed for use with unselected groups. Series B was intended for the measurement of persons believed to be musical. The latter might also be used for individual measurement. Both series measured the same capacities, but Series B was the more difficult in that it used finer increments for discrimination. Series B has since been discontinued, but the revised version of Series A still is available from The Psychological Corporation of New York City.

The Seashore measures were presented on phonograph records, each test taking one side of a 78 r.p.m. record. They now are available on a single LP record. In the revised pitch test, the listener hears a series of pairs of sounds differing in pitch. He is asked to tell whether the second sound is higher or lower than the first. The sounds were produced for recording by a General Radio beat-frequency oscillator, which permits effective control of the sound.[2] Use of tuning forks as the sound stimuli in the original pitch test had resulted in the criticism that there was a lack of uniformity in intensity and duration of the tones. The oscillator effectively eliminates this weakness, according to the authors of the revision.

---

[1]The original (1919) version of the Seashore measures bore the title, *Measures of Musical Talent*. The monograph describing the revision, the manual for the revised version published in 1940 by C. H. Stoelting Co., and subsequent manuals published by the Psychological Corporation all have used the title, *Measures of Musical Talents*.

[2]Joseph G. Saetveit, Don Lewis, and Carl E. Seashore, *Revision of the Seashore Measures of Musical Talents*. Iowa City: University of Iowa Press, 1940. p. 9.

In the description of the revision studies the authors also state that investigation had shown that some items included in the original pitch test were of little differentiating value, since they did not consistently reveal a difference between those subjects generally scoring high and those generally scoring low.[3] Such items were omitted from the revision. Since investigation had also indicated that equally satisfactory results could be obtained from a shorter pitch test, the number of items was reduced by half. The original test was subjected also to thorough item analysis, and in the revision the number of items at each level of difficulty was adjusted so as to weight the test in favor of items with the highest discriminating value. Pitch differences in the test range from two to seventeen cycles per second.

The loudness test presents the listener with pairs of sounds which differ in loudness. The subject is instructed to indicate whether the second sound is stronger (S) or weaker (W) than the first. Pitch is held constant at 440$\sim$, so that there is only one variable present. The electronic equipment used as the sound stimulus again permits effective control. The principal revision made in the loudness test was a different selection of items according to difficulty levels. Loudness increments in the test range from .5 to 4 db. The title of the test was changed from "Intensity" to "Loudness" to conform to terminology adopted by the Acoustical Society of America.

In revising the time test the authors made use of a new sound stimulus. In the original measure clicks had been used to set off unfilled intervals differing in length. Much criticism had been leveled at this type of stimulus. In the revision electronically generated pure tones are used, the listener deciding whether the second of each pair is longer (L) or shorter (S) than the first.

A similar substitution was made in revising the rhythm test. In the original, clicks had been used to present pairs of rhythm patterns, the subject deciding whether the second pattern was the same as or different from the first. In the revision, tonal pulses were used instead of clicks to create the tonal patterns.

The timbre test presents paired tones which may be the same or different in timbre. The listener is asked to tell whether the

---

[3]Ibid., p. 14.

second tone of each pair is the same as, or different from, the first in this respect. Other aspects of the sound were kept constant. Timbre was varied by altering the balance in the overtone structure of the tones used. The authors point out in their description of the test construction that they had certain doubts about the inclusion of such a measure, due to difficulties occasioned by phonograph function and room acoustics.[4] They expressed the belief that reasonably constant results might be expected but that further investigation was needed. They cautioned that particular care must be exercised in administering this test, especially in selection of phonograph and room.

In the test of tonal memory the listener hears 30 pairs of tonal patterns. In the second pattern of each pair one note is changed to make the pattern different from the first. The subject is asked to identify by number in the succession the note which is changed.

Scoring can be done by stencil or by machine. The measures are treated separately, and no attempt is made to sum or to average the scores. A "profile sheet" is made for each subject, showing that person's standing in each of the six attributes measured. Norms in deciles were provided for three levels in both the original measures and the 1939 revision. The levels are fifth and sixth grades, seventh and eighth grades, and adults. In the latest revised manual, published by the Psychological Corporation in 1956, percentile norms are given at three levels which differ slightly from the levels used in earlier tables of norms. The new norms are given for Grades 4 and 5, Grades 6, 7, and 8, and Grades 9-16.

The test manual provides clear and precise instructions for the test administrator and also for the scoring of the papers by hand or by machine. The manual also includes reliability coefficients at the three grade levels for which norms are provided. Information concerning validity is very brief, but a fairly extensive list of references from which additional information can be gained is provided. The manual includes descriptions of the tests but no information is given concerning the procedures used in designing the measures or in estimating reliability and validity, except for a statement of the senior author's beliefs with respect to validation

---

[4]Ibid., p. 24.

of the measures. Reference is made, however, to the monograph which describes the revision of the battery and which gives the procedures in detail.

According to the authors of the revised version, reliability coefficients, computed by the split-half method for each of the three levels of norms, range from .62 to .88. Difficulty in sustaining attention on the part of the subjects is thought to influence these coefficients.[5] The type of sound stimuli used may contribute to lapses of attention. This, of course, might constitute a valid criticism of the battery. Attempts to overcome this circumstance by other test authors, however, usually have resulted in a loss of control of the medium and of precision of measurement.

The 1956 revision of the test manual reports reliability coefficients at three grade levels, based on internal consistency and derived by a Kuder-Richardson formula. These coefficients range from .55 to .85. Since the formula used produces relatively conservative coefficients, these results seem generally consistent with the coefficients derived by the authors of the revised battery.

Validity of the battery is discussed in the monograph exclusively in terms of logical or content validity. The individual measures were validated by investigations of internal consistency. A number of studies have reported on the empirical validity of the original battery, using such validating criteria as grades in music courses and ratings by music teachers. Lundin[6] has summarized in table form results from several of these studies. Coefficients range from .01 to .80, with a median of .23 for pitch discrimination; from .02 to .49, with a median of .13 for intensity; from −.14 to .36 with a median of .17 for time; from −.15 to .47 with a median of .19 for rhythm; from .05 to .65 with a median of .30 for tonal memory; and from −.27 to .41 with a median of .05 for consonance. Six correlations between ratings or grades and total scores were reported by two investigators. These were −.15, .08, .08, .45, .51, and .73. The value of these studies is diminished by the probable unreliability of such validating criteria and by the fact that most of the studies were made with small and selected samples of music students.

---

[5]Ibid., p. 35.
[6]Robert W. Lundin, *An Objective Psychology of Music,* 2d ed. New York: The Ronald Press Co., 1967. p. 242.

The most extensive investigation of the validity of the Seashore *Measures of Musical Talent* was pursued at the Eastman School of Music by Hazel Stanton.[7] In this study more than two thousand students entering the preparatory and collegiate departments of the school over a ten-year period were administered the original Seashore battery. During the first five years of the investigation a test of tonal imagery also was used, and beginning in the sixth year the Iowa Comprehension Test (intelligence) was added. Scores from these tests were combined to provide five classifications into which all students were grouped. These were labeled *Discouraged, Doubtful, Possible, Probable,* and *Safe,* the terms describing the student's chances for successful completion of the course of study in the standard time period. Classifications of the students were kept from the teachers during the study in order to avoid influencing grades.

Of the group labeled Safe, 60 per cent graduated on time. Forty two per cent and 33 per cent, respectively, of the Probable and Possible groups completed the course in the prescribed time, while of the Doubtful and Discouraged classifications, only 23 per cent and 17 per cent, respectively, enjoyed like success.

Mursell[8] rejected this study as evidence of the validity of the Seashore measures on the ground that, since other criteria were used in classifying the students, results could not be attributed to the predictive value of the Seashore tests. He drew special attention to the use of the intelligence test, pointing out that it alone might have served as well as the combined measures.

In a discussion of the Stanton study and of Mursell's criticism of it, Super[9] has agreed that the study would have had greater significance as an evaluation of the predictive value of the Seashore measures if, in reporting the results, the predictive influence of the latter had been distinguished from that of the intelligence test. Basing his opinion on implications which he found in the report and

[7]Hazel M. Stanton, "The Measurement of Musical Talent." *University of Iowa Studies in the Psychology of Music,* Vol. 2, 1935.

[8]J. L. Mursell, *Psychology of Music.* New York: W. W. Norton, 1937. pp. 297-8.

[9]Donald E. Super, *Appraising Vocational Fitness By Means of Psychological Tests.* New York: Harper and Bros., 1949. p. 327.

upon an earlier study reported by Stanton, Super has suggested, however, that this investigation is of more significance in evaluating the Seashore battery than Mursell believed.

In a study not reported by Lundin, W. S. Larson found a correlation of .59 between scores on the original Seashore battery and course grades in music theory at the Eastman School of Music.[10]

An investigation of the value of the revised Seashore battery in predicting success in certain college music courses has been reported by Wilson.[11] In this study rankings of 44 students on the individual Seashore tests were correlated with grades in harmony, sight reading, and melodic dictation courses taken in the freshman year. Wilson reported significant correlations between sight reading grades and scores on the loudness and the tonal memory tests, and between dictation grades and timbre and tonal memory scores. None of the Seashore tests appeared to be a significant predictor of harmony grades. It is quite possible that the nature of this criterion, i.e., the course content, may account for lack of correlation between the test scores and the harmony grades as well as for the similar lack in other combinations.

Lundin[12] has reported correlations between scores on the pitch, rhythm, and tonal memory tests of the revised Seashore battery and ratings in melodic dictation, harmonic dictation, written harmonization, general ability in theory, vocal or instrumental performance, and a total of the first four. About one hundred college students majoring in music participated in the study. Coefficients for correlations between the criteria and the pitch test range from .13 to .32 with a median of .26; between criteria and rhythm, from .19 to .40 with a median of .33; and between criteria and tonal memory, from .23 to .45 with a median of .32. In evaluating these coefficients, as in evaluating all validity coefficients for aptitude tests, the size and selectivity of the study group should be kept in mind, as well as the nature of the criteria used.

---

[10]W. S. Larson, "Practical Experience with Music Tests," *Music Educators Journal*, 24:31, 1938.

[11]William E. Wilson, "Use of the Seashore Measures of Musical Talent in the Prediction of Certain Academic Grades for Music Students at the Pennsylvania State College." Unpublished Master's thesis, Pennsylvania State College, 1950.

[12]R. W. Lundin, "Development and Validation of a Set of Musical Ability Tests." *Psychol. Monog.*, 63:10, 1949, p. 13.

The monograph which describes the construction of the revised edition of the Seashore *Measures of Musical Talents* makes very evident the care with which the test content was chosen. Although this battery has been criticized on other grounds, there can be no question concerning the thoroughness of the procedures used in its construction.

K-D. The *K-D Music Tests,* by Jacob Kwalwasser and Peter W. Dykema, were issued in 1930. These tests take the form of a battery of ten measures, several of which purport to measure the same aptitudes as do the Seashore measures. In addition to measures of tonal memory, quality (timbre) discrimination, intensity (loudness) discrimination, time discrimination, rhythm discrimination, and pitch discrimination, the K-D battery includes measures of taste for tonal movement, melodic taste, pitch imagery, and rhythm imagery. This battery is available on records from the C. A. Gregory Company of Cincinnati.

Although the first six of these tests duplicate the functions of the Seashore measures, the approach is not always exactly the same. In the K-D measure of pitch discrimination each item consists of a tone sustained for approximately three seconds. Some tones change pitch, moving from the standard to the new pitch and back, whereas others remain constant. The subject indicates whether the pitch of the tone heard is the same throughout (S) or whether part of it is different in pitch (D). Two standard pitches, about an octave apart, are used. Each standard pitch is used for half of the test. Increments range from .01 to .40 of a tone.

The test of intensity discrimination, which is designed to measure the same capacity as that measured by the Seashore loudness test, also differs somewhat from the latter. The test consists of 30 paired comparisons, 15 pairs of single tones followed by 15 pairs of chords. The subject indicates whether the second sound is weaker (W) or stronger (S) than the first. The Duo-Art player piano was used for the sound stimulus in making the records.

In the test of time discrimination there are 25 items, each consisting of three tones produced by the Duo-Art piano. The first and third tones of each item are equal in duration, the second tone constituting the variable. In some items the second tone is as long as each of the other two, while in others it is longer by varying increments. The subject is asked to indicate whether the second tone is the same in length as the other two (S) or different from them in this respect (D).

The test of quality discrimination again presents 30 pairs of comparisons. The interval of an ascending major sixth is played twice in each item, sometimes by the same instrument both times and sometimes by two different instruments. Actual musical instruments produce the tones. The same pitch level is used throughout an item even when different instruments are used in order to limit the variables to quality (timbre) alone. The subject is asked to indicate in each item whether the intervals are played by the same instrument (S) or by different instruments (D).

The rhythm discrimination test includes 25 pairs of rhythm patterns, once again produced by the Duo-Art piano. Two pitches are used in each item, the notes b and c in the treble staff, with the pitches used in the same places in compared patterns. The variable in each case is either note duration or intensity, it being the contention of the test authors that these are the factors which constitute and condition rhythm.[13] Again the subject is asked to indicate whether the second pattern is the same as or different from the first in each item.

The tonal memory test consists of 25 items, each presenting two sequences of tones. The required response again indicates whether the two patterns in each item are the same or different.

The test of tonal movement includes 30 items, each of which consists of an obviously incomplete pattern of four tones. The subject indicates whether the tone needed to satisfactorily complete the pattern would be up (U) or down (D) from the last one heard.

The test of melodic taste measures sensitivity to structure, balance, and phrase compatibility. General musical appeal is given by the test authors as the basis for choice.[14] In this test there are ten items, each consisting of two short melodies of two phrases each. The initial phrases of the two melodies in each item are alike, but the second phrases differ from one another. The subject is asked to choose which second phrase is better, marking A or B according

---

[13]J. Kwalwasser and P. W. Dykema, *K-D Music Tests Manual of Directions.* New York: Carl Fischer, Inc., 1930. p. 14.

[14]Ibid., p. 18.

to his choice. The whole test is repeated with the instructions that the subject may make a different choice the second time but may not alter his earlier answer. In the description of the test the authors state that the subject should select the better second phrase according to congruity and compatibility as a proper termination of the first phrase, not according to the intrinsic merit of the second phrase itself.[15] In the directions to the subjects, however, no indication of this basis for selection is given.

The pitch imagery test purports to measure ability to form images of tonal effects from music notation. The subject compares 25 tonal patterns produced on the record with 25 patterns in notation on the answer sheet. He then records S or D, depending upon whether or not the pattern heard is the same as the notated pattern. The patterns vary from two notes in length to patterns of four notes separated into pairs by a rest. The authors admit that lack of facility with music notation will prove a handicap to some subjects, but it is believed that this handicap will be revealed by comparison of scores on this test with those on the tonal memory and pitch discrimination measures.[16]

The test of rhythm imagery is similar in form to that of pitch imagery. Rhythmic patterns heard on the record are compared with notated patterns on the answer sheet.

Percentile norms are given for each of the measures and for cumulative scores. Different norms are provided for three levels: Grades 4-5-6, Grades 7-8-9, and senior high school. The manual states merely that these norms are based upon scores earned by thousands of grade and high school pupils. No further information concerning the establishment of the norms is provided. The tests can be scored with the aid of cut-out stencils.

The Kwalwasser-Dykema battery has been used quite extensively by music teachers in some areas of the United States. Ease of administration and scoring, and the abundance of information which they would seem to yield within a short time, undoubtedly have contributed to their popularity, while the brevity of the individual measures has appealed to many. Many teach-

---

[15]Loc. cit.
[16]Ibid., p. 20.

ers feel that the attention of the subjects is held somewhat more successfully by these tests than by the Seashore measures because of the brevity of the separate tests and especially because actual musical sounds are used. The numbering of items on the record is another feature which appeals to some because it assists students in keeping the right place.

The test manual, unfortunately, furnishes neither reliability and validity coefficients nor reference to any source where these can be found. Independent studies which have been made of this battery, however, have consistently found that these tests have significantly lower reliability coefficients than the comparable measures of the original Seashore battery, and that in the cases of some tests reliability is so low as to question seriously the value of the test. Lundin[17] has summarized a number of studies of the reliability of the K-D measures. Coefficients given in this summary for the pitch test range from −.05 to .63 with a median of .34; from −.10 to .60 with a median of .15 for intensity; from .10 to .66 with a median of .36 for quality; from .00 to .63 with a median of .33 for time; from .04 to .48 with a median of .29 for rhythm; from .43 to .73 with a median of .55 for tonal memory; from .37 to .85 with a median of .68 for tonal movement; from .06 to .61 with a median of .35 for melodic taste; from .14 to .45 with a median of .33 for pitch imagery; and from .20 to .40 with a median of .31 for rhythm imagery.

Critics also have pointed out that most of the tests are too short and that they do not include a sufficient number of items at important discriminative levels. The tests of tonal movement and melodic taste are subject to question on the grounds that they probably measure conditioning to conventional procedures in melody writing rather than aesthetic sensitivity in music, while the tests of pitch imagery and rhythm imagery, as the authors admit, are strongly influenced by lack of facility with music notation.

Lundin[18] has summarized also the results of several studies of the validity of the Kwalwasser-Dykema battery. The criteria used in these studies included ratings of musical accomplishments and

[17]Lundin, op. cit., p. 247.
[18]Ibid., p. 248.

grades earned in various types of music study. Coefficients for the pitch test range from −.18 to .23 with a median of .00; from −.11 to .29 with a median of .13 for intensity; from −.10 to .21 with a median of .14 for quality; from −.13 to .27 with a median of .01 for time; from −.04 to .31 with a median of .16 for rhythm; from .02 to .45 with a median of .26 for tonal memory; from .00 to .31 with a median of .18 for tonal movement; from −.19 to .31 with a median of .01 for melodic taste; from .00 to .59 with a median of .31 for pitch imagery; and from .01 to .46 with a median of .29 for rhythm imagery. One investigator, using two different criteria, reported coefficients of .02 and .16 for total scores.

These coefficients, too, are in general lower than those found in investigations of the original Seashore battery. As with the Seashore battery, however, the nature of the validating criteria and the size and selectivity of the participating groups should be kept in mind in evaluating the coefficients. From the information available, the validating studies seem to have been comparable to those made of the original Seashore battery.

Tilson-Gretsch. The *Tilson-Gretsch Musical Aptitude Tests,* authored by Lowell Mason Tilson, were copyrighted in 1941 by the Fred Gretsch Manufacturing Company. These tests are not available commercially but usually are administered upon request by a company representative as a service to music education. This battery is somewhat similar to Seashore and to at least part of the K-D battery in general approach. The battery includes four measures; one each of pitch discrimination, intensity discrimination, time discrimination, and tonal memory.

The pitch discrimination test presents 25 pairs of pitches, the subjects indicating whether the second tone of each pair is higher or lower than the first. A reed instrument which, according to the test manual, the test author found in the science laboratory at Indiana State Teachers College, Terre Haute, Indiana, was used as the sound stimulus for this test. The items are constructed around a pitch of 440, with increments ranging from twenty vibrations to four vibrations per second.

The intensity test also consists of 25 items, each a pair of sounds differing in loudness. An audiometer was used as the sound stimulus, and the differences in intensity range from ten decibels to one decibel. The subject indicates whether the second sound in each item is stronger or weaker than the first.

In the time test, 25 pairs of tones differing in length by increments ranging from one-fifth of a second to four-fifths of a second are presented. The subject indicates whether the second is longer or shorter than the first. The audiometer serves as the sound stimulus, and a metronome was used as a timing device.

Like the other three tests in the battery, the tonal memory test consists of 25 items. These are pairs of tonal patterns, ranging in length from three tones to six, played on an electric organ. The subject is asked to identify by number the tone which has been changed in the second pattern of each item.

Answer sheets are prepared so that the subject must merely make a check under the right answer. To some, this is preferable to both the old Seashore and the K-D answer sheets in which the subject must write the appropriate letter for the answer. Since the Seashore measures now have been provided with machine scored answer blanks, they no longer suffer from comparison on this point. Instructions are given on the record, ensuring uniformity but making it more difficult to be certain that all subjects understand clearly what they are to do.

These tests also can be scored with stencils, and the table of norms is printed in the margin of the scoring stencil. This is a convenience in ranking papers. Norms are given in percentiles for three levels; Grades 4-6, Grades 7-9, and Grades 10-12. The norms are given, however, only for totaled scores.

The Tilson-Gretsch test manual, which actually is a reprint of an article which appeared in the May, 1941, issue of *The Teachers College Journal*, provides information concerning reliability and validity as well as a description of procedures used in constructing the test battery. Reliability coefficients, derived by the retest method range from .44+ to .72+ for the separate measures. A reliability coefficient of .83+, derived by the same method, for the entire battery also is given.

According to the author these tests were constructed for use in the elementary and secondary schools.[19] He disclaims any inten-

---

[19]L. M. Tilson, "A Study of the Prognostic Value of the Tilson-Gretsch Musical Aptitude Tests." *The Teachers College Journal*, May, 1941.

tion of producing a battery sensitive enough for the selection of students for college music education curricula. This undoubtedly is the reason why these measures do not make use of as fine discriminating elements as do the Seashore measures.

Unfortunately, little information from independent studies of the reliability and validity of these tests is available. Farnsworth[20] has criticized the low difficulty level of the test items, and he has found the battery generally inferior to the revised Seashore measures.

Drake. The *Drake Musical Aptitude Tests,* by Raleigh M. Drake, include tests of musical memory and rhythm. These measures currently are available on records from Science Research Associates of Chicago.

The musical memory test is the same as that which has been available separately for a number of years. Two forms of equivalent difficulty are provided, each including 12 items. Each item, or trial, consists of a short melody with which the subject is to compare a number of other melodies. The number of comparisons increases from two in each of the first two trials to seven in each of the last two. In each trial the standard melody is *not* repeated between comparisons. Each comparison may be exactly the same as the standard or it may be changed in one of three ways. It may be played in a different key; a change may be made in time values of constituent notes, or one or more pitches may be changed. The subject responds by writing S, K, T, or N according to his judgment of the comparison.

The rhythm test also has two forms, but these are not equivalent in difficulty. Form A sets up a pulse, or beat, which the subject is to continue counting in time after the stimulus has ceased. Counting consecutively, the subject then answers by recording the number which he has reached when given the command to stop. Form B similarly sets up a pulse which the subject is to maintain, but in this form of the test the subject must continue to count the pulse against a distracting beat. He answers in the same manner as in Form A.

Items are numbered on the records, a desirable practice when working with children, and separate practice items are provided.

---

[20]Paul R. Farnsworth. *The Social Psychology of Music,* 2d ed. Ames, Iowa: The Iowa State University Press, 1969. pp. 195-6.

The test manual provides clear and explicit instructions for administering and scoring the test, and it includes satisfactory data concerning reliability and validity. Split-half reliability coefficients for combined A and B forms of the musical memory test were computed separately for a group of 178 students with less than five years of musical training and two much smaller groups of students with five or more years of musical training. The coefficient for the first group was .85, and those for the two smaller groups were .91 and .93. Several coefficients, computed by split-half and Kuder-Richardson techniques, are given for each of the rhythm tests. Those for Form A range from .56 to .95 with a median of .86. For Form B the range is from .69 to .96 with a median of .775.

Validity coefficients have been computed by correlating test scores with ratings of expression in playing and rapidity in learning music. For the combined forms of the musical memory test these coefficients range from .32 to .91 with a median of .55. The range for Form A of the rhythm test is from .31 to .82 with a median of .585, and for Form B the range is from .41 to .83 with a median of .67. The combined forms of the rhythm test produced coefficients ranging from .31 to .85 with a median of .58.

Again, it is unfortunate that no information concerning the reliability and validity of these tests is available from independent studies. This lack makes quite evident the need for further research in this area.

Whistler-Thorpe. The *Musical Aptitude Test,* devised by Harvey S. Whistler and Louis P. Thorpe and published in 1950 by the California Test Bureau, is divided into five sections. The sections are entitled Rhythm Recognition, Pitch Recognition, Melody Recognition, Pitch Discrimination, and Advanced Rhythm Recognition.

The Rhythm Recognition section consists of ten items, each containing a pair of rhythm patterns. The subject is to indicate in each case whether the second pattern is the same as, or different from, the first.

The Pitch Recognition section also contains ten items. Each consists of a four measure melody in quarter notes in $\frac{4}{4}$ meter. Before the melody is presented, a single tone is played. Then the subject is to indicate the number of times that particular pitch appears in the melody which follows.

The Melody Recognition section consists of 25 pairs of melodic patterns, each two measures in length. The subject is asked to indicate whether the second pattern in each pair is the same as, or different from, the first. Differences may be tonal or rhythmic, but no distinction is asked of the subject.

In the Pitch Discrimination section the subject hears 15 pairs of chords. Ten items consist of three note chords, while in the last five items the lowest note of the chord is duplicated at the octave above, thus producing a cluster of four pitches. The subject is asked to indicate whether the second chord of each pair is the same as, higher than, or lower than, the first. When "same" is expected for the answer the original chord is repeated. When "higher" or "lower" is expected, two different chords are presented. In one or two cases the different chords are of the same type, i.e., major, minor, etc., but in most items the two chords used are of different types. In a few cases the two different chords have a common lowest tone, although it may be spelled enharmonically.

The Advanced Rhythm Recognition Test is very similar to the first test, Rhythm Recognition. The advanced test contains 15 items, each a pair of rhythmic patterns which are to be compared. Once again, the subject is to indicate whether the second of the pair is the same as, or different from, the first. A few items in the Advanced Rhythm test used slightly more intricate rhythms, e.g., dotted eighth and sixteenth, and triplet in $\frac{4}{4}$ meter, than are used in the first Rhythm Recognition test. The majority of the items, however, seem no more complex or difficult than those of the earlier test.

The test is administered from the piano. IBM answer sheets, which can be scored either by machine or by hand with the use of a stencil, are used. The test is designed for use in grades four through ten. Percentile norms are provided for each grade from four through eight, with one table for grades nine and ten. The test manual provides adequate directions for the administration of the test and clear instructions to be given to the subjects. It also provides satisfactory information concerning reliability and validity studies.

Reliability is expressed separately in both indexes of reliability and reliability coefficients derived by the Kuder-Richardson formula for rhythm (presumably combining parts one and five of the test), pitch (presumably combining parts two and four), melody, and total score. Indexes of reliability (see Chapter 4) range from .80 for rhythm to .93 for total score. The corresponding coefficients of reliability range from .64 to .87.

Validity coefficients obtained by correlating one hundred test scores with teachers' ratings of instrumental and vocal talent and with participation in musical groups range from .19 to .56. The authors also claim "face" validity for the measures on the ground that the elements measured are basic elements of musical aptitude.[21]

Little information derived from independent studies of the reliability and validity of the Whistler-Thorpe tests is available. Bentley[22] has reported a reliability coefficient, obtained by the use of the Kuder-Richardson formula with two hundred cases, of .745 for total scores. He has reported also a validity coefficient obtained by correlating test scores with grades in music courses. The courses are not identified or described. For a group of about two hundred high school students, divided about evenly between those currently participating in instrumental groups and those not currently participating, a coefficient of .379 was obtained.

Some readers may question the validity of some statements made in the introductory section of the manual. The use of no pitch differences smaller than the semitone is justified there, for example, on the ground that, because composers do not use finer differences, they are not required in real music situations. While it is quite true that the system of tonal organization in which most of the music of the past three centuries has been conceived does not make use of intervals smaller than the semitone, it does not follow that finer degrees of discrimination are not important in real music situations. It hardly need be pointed out that accurate intonation in performance requires much finer discrimination.

Kwalwasser. Jacob Kwalwasser, co-author of the *Kwalwasser-Dykema Music Tests,* also is author of a newer test published in 1953 by the Mills Music Company. This test, known as the *Kwal-*

21H. S. Whistler and L. P. Thorpe, *Musical Aptitude Test, Series A.* Hollywood, Calif.: California Test Bureau, 1950. p. 7.

22R. R. Bentley, "A Critical Comparison of Certain Music Aptitude Tests." Doctoral Dissertation, published on microfilm, University of Southern California, 1955. p. 271.

wasser Music Talent Test, is available in two forms, each on one ten-inch 78 r.p.m. phonograph record. The forms are not equivalent in difficulty or in length. Form A consists of 50 items, and it is designed for use in grades seven and above. Form B includes 40 items and is an easier form designed for use in grades four through six. The content of both forms is similar in nature.

The test items consist of pairs of short melodic patterns. In each pair the second pattern differs from the first in pitch, time, rhythm, or loudness. On the answer blank the subject may select one of two possible answers which are chosen from these four possible methods of variation. In an item in which the rhythm of the pattern is changed, for example, the subject may be asked to decide whether the change is in rhythm or pitch. There always is a change, and in each item the subject has the choice of two answers.

Separate norms are provided at three levels. Form B is accompanied by norms for grades four through six. Form A provides two sets of norms, one for junior high school and the other for senior high and college levels.

The test manual provides neither standard directions for administration of the test nor data concerning reliability and validity. No information concerning the construction of the test is given, and no reference is made to any source for such information.

Information concerning reliability and validity, therefore, is very scant. Farnsworth[23], using 55 college students, found a split-half coefficient of .48 for the test. Bentley[24] also has reported on the reliability of the *Kwalwasser Music Talent Test* as well as upon its validity. Using a Kuder-Richardson formula, he obtained a reliability coefficient of .591 for approximately two hundred cases. Using the same number of high school students, Bentley found a correlation of .456 between scores on the test and grades attained in music courses.

The test is short and it can be administered in a brief period. It would seem, however, that brevity has been gained at the cost of reliability and of balance in discriminating levels among the

[23]Oscar K. Buros (ed.), *Fifth Mental Measurements Yearbook.* Highland Park, N.J.: Gryphon Press, 1959. pp. 383-4.

[24]Bentley, op. cit., p. 271.

items. The lack of information concerning reliability and validity understandably has provoked strong criticism.

Gaston. Another musical aptitude test of relatively recent publication is the *Test of Musicality* by E. Thayer Gaston. This test is available in its fourth edition from Odell's Instrumental Service of Lawrence, Kansas.

The test includes 40 items, only 39 of which are scored. The first 17 items constitute an interest inventory, asking questions concerning use of music in the home, attitude of other members of the subject's family toward music, interest in musical organizations and other types of activity, etc. Item 18 asks the subject to list in order the instruments which he would like to play.

Of the remaining 22 items, which are recorded with instructions on one LP record, five measure ability to find a given tone in a chord. The subject checks either "Yes" or "No" on the answer sheet. Five items measure ability to detect differences of note or rhythm between melodic patterns in notation on the answer blank and those which the subject hears on the record. Possible answers are "Same," "Note," and "Rhythm." Five more items consist of short melodic phrases lacking final notes. The subject is asked to indicate in each case whether the final note should be higher or lower than the last one played. In the last seven items a melody is presented with a number of comparisons. The subject is to indicate in the case of each comparison whether it is the same as the standard, whether a change in notes has been made, or whether a change in rhythm has been effected. The number of comparisons increases progressively from two to six, and the standard melody is not repeated between comparisons.

A piano was used to produce the items for the recording. All answers are recorded by placing check marks in appropriate blanks. The test is provided with a cut-out stencil for hand scoring but at this time it cannot be scored by machine.

The last page of the test blank provides space for the notation of data concerning the pupil's voice register, ability to perform on an instrument, and I.Q. This is to be filled in by the teacher before the earlier parts of the test are scored, so as to avoid contamination of the ratings.

The manual for the Gaston *Test of Musicality* provides explicit instructions for the administration and scoring of the test. Norms, in the form of Otis Percentile Charts,[25] are given separately for page one of the test blank (the interest inventory) and for pages two and three (the recorded section of the test). For page one norms are given separately for girls at two levels (grades 4-8 and grades 9-12) and for boys at the same two levels. For pages two and three norms again are given separately for boys and girls, this time at five levels (grade 4, grades 5 and 6, grades 7 and 8, grades 9 and 10, and grades 11 and 12). A total of nearly six thousand cases was used in the derivation of the norms.

Reliability coefficients, computed by the split-half method, are provided at three levels: Grades 4-6, 7-9, and 10-12. A coefficient of .88 is given for each of the first two levels, and one of .90 for the last. Validity was estimated by an unusual statistical technique which undoubtedly is not clear to many readers of the manual, but the author states that the results indicate that the test is a valid measure of what it purports to measure.[26] The manual does not explain whether or not the first 17 items, which comprise the interest inventory, were included in the investigation of reliability and validity.

Bentley[27] has reported a Kuder-Richardson reliability coefficient of .839 for the *Test of Musicality*. In the same study, this investigator obtained a correlation of .522 between scores attained on this test by approximately two hundred high school students and grades in music courses.

One might question whether sections of only five items each, especially those in which the subject is given the option of only two answers for each item, contribute significantly to the value of the test. Perhaps further research with this test will provide a satisfactory answer to the question. The section which requires the subject to suggest the direction for a concluding note in a pattern also is open to the same questions which may be directed at any test which purports to measure taste in this way.

Wing. A significant contribution to the bibliography of musical aptitude measures was made in 1939 by an English educator,

[25]Otis Percentile Chart, Copyright 1938 by World Book Company, Yonkers-on-Hudson, New York.

[26]E. Thayer Gaston, *A Test of Musicality, Manual of Directions, Fourth Edition, Revised*. Lawrence, Kansas: Odell's Instrumental Service, 1957. pp. 4-5.

[27]Bentley, op. cit., p. 271.

Herbert Wing. This was the *Wing Standardized Tests of Musical Intelligence,* a battery of seven tests which deal with chord analysis, pitch change, memory, rhythmic accent, harmony, intensity, and phrasing. This battery appeared on records after World War II, and in 1958 a revised edition was issued on tape.

The theoretical bases of the tests and the procedures used in constructing them are described in detail in the *British Journal of Psychology Monographs Supplement* XXVII entitled, "Tests of Musical Ability and Appreciation," by Herbert Wing. The tests obviously are the result of careful and thorough investigation on the part of their author.

In the chord analysis test both single notes and chords are struck. The subject is asked to indicate the number of notes played in each of the 20 items. In the pitch change measure, the subject is required to detect a change of pitch when two chords are played successively. The two chords may be identical, or one note may move up or down in progressing from the first chord to the second. The subject responds "S," "U," or "D," according to his decision as to whether the chords are the same or whether one note moves up or down. This test includes 30 items.

The memory test presents 30 pairs of melodic patterns ranging in length from three notes to ten. The second pattern of each pair may be the same as the first, or one note may be changed. If the subject finds the two patterns identical, he writes an "S" in the space provided. If a note is changed he indicates the number of that note in the progression.

The four tests remaining measure taste as well as perception. In the test of rhythmic accent, each of the 14 items consists of two renditions of the same tune. In some items the two renditions are exactly the same; in some, accents are relocated in the second playing to give it a different rhythmic effect. If the two are the same, the subject should write in an "S." If the two are different, he should indicate his preference between them by writing in either "A" or "B."

The test of harmony is similar in principle. In this test, however, the harmonization of the melody is the variable. Again the subject may write in an "S" to indicate that the two renditions are the same. If they are different, he may indicate his preference by writing in either "A" or "B." This test also has 14 items.

In the intensity test dynamic relationships within the tune constitute the variable. In some items the two renditions of the tune are alike. In others, louder and softer portions are relocated in the second playing. The subject again has the choice of three answers— "S," "A," and "B"—for each of the 14 items.

In the final test, phrasing, the variable is the phrase grouping. Again there are 14 items, each consisting of two playings of the same tune. Once more the subject indicates whether they are the same or, if not, his preference between the two.

The Wing *Standardized Tests of Musical Intelligence* may be used at age seven and above. Norms are provided for age eight and above in terms of a five letter grade scale based on a 10 per cent—20 per cent—40 per cent—20 per cent—10 per cent distribution. It has been suggested that the first three tests of the battery might be used alone to reduce the amount of time required for testing, and Wing proposes such a step when testing young children.

Wing reports reliability coefficients ranging from .70 to .90 for different age levels for totaled scores. McLeish[28], in a review of these tests, reports a split-half reliability coefficient of .90 for totaled scores attained by a group of one hundred adults. Using the same group he obtained reliability coefficients ranging from .65 to .86 for the individual tests, a range below that which he found for the separate tests of the Seashore battery. Bentley[29], using a Kuder-Richardson formula with about two hundred high school students, obtained a reliability coefficient of .857, also for totaled scores.

The manual states that correlation of the tests with another (Aliferis; pages 162-164), using college students as subjects, gave a coefficient of .73 which, when corrected for attenuation, would rise to .90. When scores attained by considerably younger subjects were correlated with teacher ratings a coefficient of .60 was obtained. Using an earlier version of the tests, Wing found some relationship between test standings, expressed in a three level grouping, and drop-outs from instrumental instruction.[30] Further

[28]Oscar K. Buros (ed.), *Fourth Mental Measurements Yearbook*. Highland Park, N.J.: Gryphon Press, 1953. p. 345.

[29]Bentley, op. cit., p. 271.

[30]Herbert Wing, "Tests of Musical Ability and Appreciation." *Brit. J. Psychol. Monog. Suppl.*, XVII, 1948. p. 73.

empirical estimation of validity of the Wing tests has been offered by Bentley[31], who obtained a validity coefficient of .481 by correlating totaled scores with grades earned in music courses.

Scores for this battery are recorded for the individual tests as well as for totaled scores. The revised edition included scoring stencils which facilitate manual marking of the answer papers and thus overcome an earlier minor criticism. An IBM answer sheet which permits machine scoring is now available.

Gordon. Published in 1965 by the Houghton Mifflin Company, the *Musical Aptitude Profile* by Edwin Gordon consists of three tests: Tonal Imagery, Rhythm Imagery, and Musical Sensitivity.

The Tonal Imagery test is divided into two sections, Tonal Imagery—Melody and Tonal Imagery—Harmony, each of which contains forty items. Each item presents a short musical statement or "song," as it is called in the test instructions, and an answer. In the Melody section the answer always contains more notes than the song and may be an embellished variant of the latter or more noticeably different from it. If the answer is a variant of the song the correct response is "like"; if it is not a variant the response should be "different." If the test subject cannot decide, he may indicate his doubt, thus eliminating the necessity to guess. All items in this section of the test are played on a violin.

The Tonal Imagery-Harmony test is similar in that each item presents a comparison of a statement, or "song," and an answer. Each has two musical lines, played by a violin and 'cello duo. The upper line always is the same in both song and answer, but the lower line of the answer may be a harmonic variant of that of the song or may be harmonically different from it. Again, the test subject may respond "like," "different," or "in doubt" by filling in the appropriate space on the answer sheet.

The Rhythm Imagery test also is divided into two sections, each containing forty items performed on a violin. Each item again presents a selection and an answer, both of which in this case have the same melodic contour. In the first section of the test, Rhythm Imagery-Tempo, the variable is the tempo of the

---

[31]Bentley, op. cit., p. 301.

music. The selection and answer may be exactly alike or the tempo of the answer may be either speeded up or slowed down toward the end. Again the response may be "like," "different," or "in doubt."

In the second section of the Rhythm Imagery test, Rhythm Imagery-Meter, the variable is the metrical structure of the melody. The answer to a statement or song may be in the same meter as the latter or its metrical structure may be different. As in the earlier sections of the *Profile,* the subject may respond "like," "different," or "in doubt."

The third test of the *Musical Aptitude Profile* is entitled Musical Sensitivity. It is in three sections—Phrasing, Balance, and Style—each of which contains thirty items.

In the Musical Sensitivity-Phrasing test each item consists of a short musical selection or statement with two lines, played twice by a violin and 'cello duo. The two renditions of the short statement are identical except that the phrasing is altered in the second. The subject is asked to indicate which rendition he considers to be better or to indicate if he cannot decide.

Each item of the Musical Sensitivity-Balance test consists of a short musical statement followed by a partial repetition but with a different ending, both played by a violin. The respondent is asked which ending he considers better. Again he may indicate doubt if he cannot decide.

In the Musical Sensitivity-Style test each item again consists of two renditions of a short melodic statement played by a violin. The two renditions are performed at different tempi, thus varying the style. In this test, too, the subject is asked to indicate his preference between the two renditions or to express his doubt.

The musical selections used in the three tests of the *Musical Aptitude Profile* were composed by the test author, Edwin Gordon. As the test manual points out, the use of originally composed selections ensures that no test subjects are likely to be familiar with the music used.[32] The entire battery, including instructions to the subjects, is recorded on magnetic tape. Performance, instructions, and technical quality of the tapes are

---

[32]Edwin Gordon, *Manual Musical Aptitude Profile.* Boston: Houghton Mifflin Co., 1965, p. 6.

excellent. The tests can be scored manually with the aid of stencils provided with the test materials or they may be sent to the Houghton Mifflin Scoring Service for electronic processing. The manual provided gives information about the rationale and development of the tests, directions for organizing and administering the test program, comments on the interpretation and use of test results, and copious data about the standardization procedures used.

Reliability coefficients derived through split-half procedures are given separately for each of nine grade levels (4-12) for each of the seven subtests, each of the three tests, and for the composite score on the entire *Profile*. Additional reliability coefficients are given for the same subdivisions for musically select subjects at three levels, grades 4-6, grades 7-9, and grades 10-12. Coefficients for the seven subtests using the total standardization sample range from .66 to .85; those for the three main tests from .80 to .92; and those for the composite score from .90 to .96. Comparable coefficients for musically select subjects range from .70 to .84, from .83 to .90, and from .93 to .95, respectively.

The manual also includes a discussion of the validity of the tests. Concurrent criterion-related validity coefficients, using teachers' ratings of musical talent as the validating criteria, for the three tests and seven subtests and for composite scores are cited. These range from .19 to .97, with those for composite scores and the three main tests lying generally in the .60's and .70's. Coefficients for composite scores, using subjective judgments of musical performance as the validating criteria, range somewhat lower as one might expect. In view of the difficulties inherent in such methods of validation, as discussed in Chapter 7, these coefficients are not unimpressive.

The manual provides a table for conversion of raw scores to standard scores as do the scoring stencils, and percentile norms are provided separately for all standard scores on the tests at the nine grade levels for unselected students (4-12) and for the three levels of musically select students (grades 4-6, 7-9, 10-12). Norms for use with college freshman music students have been suggested in a study by Lee.[33]

---

[33]Robert Edward Lee, "An Investigation of the Use of the Musical Aptitude Profile with College and University Freshman Music Students." Unpublished Doctoral Dissertation, University of Iowa, 1966.

Additional evidence of validity of the *Musical Aptitude Profile* has been provided by Gordon through a three year longitudinal predictive study.[34] In this study scores on the *Musical Aptitude Profile* were correlated after an intervening three year period of musical training with judges' ratings of students' musical performances, teachers' evaluations of student achievement in instrumental music, and students' scores on a music achievement test. Correlations between individual subtests of the *Profile* and individual criteria range from .17 to .56, and those between the composite score of the *Profile* and individual criteria from .35 to .71. The correlation between the composite score on the *Profile* and a grand composite of criterion scores was .75. These coefficients for the *Profile* composite score compare favorably with those generally reported for general academic and vocational aptitude tests.

The *Musical Aptitude Profile* was developed and standardized through careful and thorough procedures, and its construction is technically sound. Some may question the suitability of some of the test titles and, as the author admits in the test manual,[35] some of the terminology used may seem inaccurate to subjects who have some familiarity with such terms as "phrasing," "balance," and "style." The instructions are clear, however, and with the practice exercises they should overcome any lack of accuracy in terminology. The question of the terminology thus does not seem important. As with other tests, additional studies of reliability, validity, and applicability of the *Musical Aptitude Profile* are needed. In the light of experience to date, however, it is apparent that the battery constitutes an outstanding contribution to the field of musical aptitude testing.

Bentley. The *Measures of Musical Ability* by Arnold Bentley are designed for use with children of ages seven through fourteen, thus reaching a lower age level than any other published measure of musical aptitude or achievement. The battery consists of four tests: pitch discrimination (called simply "Pitch" in the instructions and on the answer form), tonal memory (called

---

[34]Edwin Gordon, *A Three Year Study of the Musical Aptitude Profile.* Iowa City: University of Iowa Press, 1967.

[35]Gordon, *Manual,* p. 12.

"Tunes"), chord analysis (called "Chords"), and rhythmic memory (called "Rhythm").

The pitch discrimination test consists of thirty items, each of which presents a pair of tones, played successively, for comparison. The second tone of each item may be the same as, higher than, or lower than the first. The first tone of each item has a vibration frequency of 440 c.p.s., and differences in pitch range from a semitone down to approximately three twenty sixths of a semitone. The test subject is instructed to answer "S" if the second tone is the same as the first; "U" if the second sound "goes up" (i.e., is higher than the first); and "D" if the second sound "goes down," or is lower than the first. Sine wave oscillators were used as the sound stimulus for this test.

The tonal memory test consists of ten items, each presenting a pair of five note tunes. Subjects are asked to compare the tunes in each item, responding "S" if they are the same or identifying by number the changed note if they are not the same. Discrepancies between the tunes are in pitch only; no rhythmic alterations are made. The rhythm of the tunes is very simple, consisting of five notes of equal duration played at a constant speed of approximately 120 per minute. A pipe organ was used as the medium of performance.

The chord analysis test contains twenty items. Each presents a chord, played harmonically, consisting of two, three, or four tones. The test subjects are asked to indicate how many tones are present in each chord. The chords are played on a pipe organ.

The final test of the battery, that of rhythmic memory, contains ten items. Each item consists of a pair of four note rhythmic patterns, played at a constant pitch on a pipe organ. The subjects are asked to respond "S" if the two patterns in an item are the same, or with the number of the pulse in which a change occurs. Although pitch is held constant throughout an item, each item is played at a different pitch in an attempt to relieve monotony.

Information concerning the development of the *Measures of Musical Ability* and the reliability and validity of the battery is given in detail in Bentley's book *Musical Ability in Children and Its Measurement*.[36] Reliability was determined by the test author

---

[36]Arnold Bentley, *Musical Ability in Children and Its Measurement*. London: George G. Harrap & Co. Ltd., 1966.

through the re-test method with a group of 90 children ranging in age from 9 years 10 months to 11 years 9 months. The coefficient derived was .84. Validity was studied through comparison of test scores with class teachers' estimates of musical ability, progress in some musical activity, performance on examinations for choral scholarships, and grades in an examination in music class work. The test also was administered to 160 individuals who already had demonstrated accomplishment in some form of musical pursuit. These studies indicate a positive association between the test scores and the criteria with which they were compared. Further studies by other researchers are needed, however, to provide additional information about the reliability and validity of the Bentley *Measures*. Since the unique feature of this battery is its intended application at lower age levels, there is a particular need for further study of reliability and validity with children in the seven to nine year age levels.

Bentley's book, which serves effectively as a manual for the battery, also provides instructions for administration and suggestions for interpretation of test results. Norms, in terms of a five letter grade scale similar to that used by Wing, are provided for ages seven through fourteen. It would be advisable for any prospective user of the Bentley battery to read this book carefully, although a six page leaflet is provided with the test materials as a brief manual.

The test battery is recorded on a ten-inch long playing record, complete with instructions and examples. The recording is of good quality. The *Measures of Musical Ability* are published by George G. Harrap and Company Ltd. of London, publishers of Bentley's book.

Unpublished Measures of Musical Aptitude. Other measures pertaining to musical aptitude and ability have been devised by Lowery, Schoen, Ortmann, Madison, and Lundin. These have been described by their authors in articles and monographs, although the measures themselves have not appeared in published form.

Lowery[37, 38] included three tests. These purport to measure musical memory, judgment of finality effects of cadences, and

---

[37]H. Lowery, "Cadence and Phrase Tests of Musical Talent." *Brit. J. Psychol.*, 17, 1926.
[38]H. Lowery, "Musical Memory." *Brit. J. Psychol.*, 19, 1929.

ability to detect changes in phrasing. In the cadence test the subject is asked to judge which of two cadences is more complete. In the phrasing test a melodic pattern is repeated with either the same or different phrase groupings, the subject indicating whether or not the two are the same or different. In the memory test an initial phrase is followed by several others, some of which are modifications of the original. The subject indicates in the case of each phrase whether or not it is based on the original.

The battery devised by Schoen[39] included three measures, one each of relative pitch (interval discrimination), tonal sequence, and rhythm. In the test of relative pitch the subject compares two intervals in pitch, judging whether the second is smaller or larger than the first. Each item of the test of tonal sequence presents an opening phrase followed by four alternative concluding phrases. The subject is required to rate the four alternative conclusions according to appropriateness. The rhythm test presents 25 pairs of rhythmic phrases, each phrase containing two rhythmic patterns which may or may not be exactly alike. Rhythm is isolated from pitch in this test. The subject is asked to judge whether the second phrase is the same as or different from the first and, if different, whether the change occurs in the first or in the second pattern of the second phrase.

Ortmann[40] included tests of pitch discrimination, pitch memory, time discrimination, fusion, rhythm memory, melodic memory, and harmonic memory. The pitch discrimination test presents 50 pairs of tones, the subject indicating whether the second of each pair is higher or lower than the first. The pitch memory test consists of five series of tones. Each tone is to be judged as higher than, lower than, or the same as, a standard tone which is given at the beginning of the series. In the test of time discrimination the second pattern of each of 50 pairs of rhythmic patterns is to be rated as more even or more uneven than the first. In this test, too, the rhythmic aspect of music is isolated from the tonal, the patterns being presented in clicks. The fusion test presents five tonal

[39]Max Schoen, "Tests of Musical Feeling and Understanding." *J. Comp. Psychol.*, 5, 1925; pp. 31-52.

[40]O. Ortmann, "Tests of Musical Talent." Peabody Conservatory of Music, unpublished. For a description, see Schoen, *Psychology of Music*, pp. 180-1.

clusters ranging in number from two to four tones and varying in degree of fusion. The subject is asked to judge the number of tones in each clang. The test of rhythm memory consists of five series of rhythmic patterns, again presented in clicks. In each series the subsequent patterns are compared with the standard, and each is rated as more even or more uneven than, or the same as, the standard. Melodic memory is measured by 25 pairs of melodies, ranging in length from two to six tones. In each pair the subject is to identify the tones which have been changed in the second melody. The harmonic memory test presents five series of chords, each consisting of a standard and a number of comparisons. Each comparison is to be judged either the same as or different from the standard.

Madison[41] approached the measurement of aptitude through what he actually believes to be a measure of achievement. His extensive studies of interval discrimination resulted in construction of a measure of this ability which has been found to correlate significantly with grades in music theory and with indexes of musical ability at the secondary school level.

Lundin[42] presented a battery of five tests in 1949. These include measures of interval discrimination, melodic transposition, mode discrimination, melodic sequences, and rhythmic sequences. The interval discrimination test presents 50 pairs of intervals played melodically, 25 ascending and 25 descending. The subject is to indicate whether the second interval in each pair is the same as, or different from, the second. The test of melodic transposition consists of 30 pairs of melodies. The second of each pair may be an exact replica of the first but in a different key, or one or more notes as well as the key may be changed in the second melody. If only the key is changed the subject should answer "S" for same. If any note relationships within the melody are changed the correct response is "D" for different. In the test of mode discrimination 30 pairs of single chords are presented. The subject is to indicate whether the two chords in each pair are the same or dif-

---

[41]T. H. Madison, "Interval Discrimination As a Measure of Musical Aptitude." *Arch. Psychol.*, No. 268, 1942.

[42]R. W. Lundin, "The Development and Validation of A Set of Musical Ability Tests," *Psychol. Monog.*, 63:10, 1949.

ferent in internal structure, i.e., whether or not they both are major triads or minor triads, etc. The melodic sequences test includes 30 items, each of which consists of four melodic patterns. If the fourth is a true sequential continuation of the first three, which are always truly sequential in a key, the subject responds with an "S." If the fourth pattern in the group is not a true sequential continuation of the first three, the correct response is "D." The rhythmic sequences test is very similar, except that the subject answers on the basis of rhythmic relationship instead of tonal. The rhythm patterns are given tonal contours, however, so that rhythm is not isolated from the pitch element in melody.

Lundin computed reliability coefficients by the split-half method using a group of 167 college music students and a group of 196 unselected college students. With the selected group, coefficients for the five separate tests ranged from .60 to .79 with a coefficient of .89 for totaled scores. With the unselected group, the coefficients for four of the tests ranged from .71 to .77, with a coefficient of .10 for the mode discrimination test and of .85 for total scores.

Validity was estimated by correlating scores attained by the music students with teacher ratings in melodic dictation, harmonic dictation, written harmonization, general ability in music theory, and performance. Only 62 students were rated on performance. Correlations between individual tests and separate ratings ranged from .10 for written harmony and rhythmic sequences to .66 for melodic dictation and interval discrimination. The range of coefficients for total test scores and separate ratings ranged from .43 to .70; for total ratings and individual tests from .26 to .68; and the coefficient for total scores and total ratings was .69. The unselected students were not used in the validation study since the author had available no appropriate criteria with which to correlate test scores.

Many manufacturers and retailers of musical instruments present their own measures of "musical talent." Some of these have been constructed with some care and with at least some attempt at logical validity. Far more, however, appear to have been inspired principally by commercial considerations with no regard for scientific procedures in test construction. Few present any satisfactory data on construction and standardization procedures, and most lack information concerning reliability and validity. Few of them actually have been standardized.

The careful teacher will examine any such tests for the requirements set forth in earlier chapters and will evaluate these measures accordingly. He will be especially wary of tests which are administered or scored by a commercial organization other than those established specifically for electronic processing of test materials. Generally he will be more satisfied with a test which he scores himself or which can be sent to a reputable testing agency for machine scoring, despite the time and effort which others might offer to save him.

Summary

Ten published measures of musical aptitude have been described in this chapter. The titles and publishers of these tests are listed following.

Other measures have been constructed and described by Lowery, Schoen, Ortmann, Madison, and Lundin. These tests have not appeared in published form.

A number of manufacturers and retailers of musical instruments also have presented measures of "musical talent." Most of these have not been standardized, and many are of questionable background. Teachers should scrutinize such tests very carefully before considering their use.

Most of the available measures possess certain virtues and have certain faults. The music teacher or counselor should weigh measures according to the evaluative criteria listed in Chapter 4. Some tests are easier to administer and score than others. Some seem superior in theoretical basis or methods of construction. It should be kept in mind, however, that scientific procedure in construction, resulting in satisfactory reliability and validity and in significant differentiating power, is an absolute essential. Lack of these qualities cannot be compensated for by any advantages in ease of administration and scoring, economy, student interest, or the like, even though all are valuable additional qualities. If information giving assurance of sound scientific procedure, reliability, and validity is not readily available, the value of any measure inevitably is in doubt.

MUSICAL APTITUDE MEASURES DESCRIBED IN THIS CHAPTER

Drake Musical Aptitude Test, by Raleigh M. Drake. Published by Science Research Associates, Inc.

K-D Music Tests, by Jacob Kwalwasser and Peter W. Dykema. Published by Carl Fischer, Inc.

Kwalwasser Music Talent Test, by Jacob Kwalwasser. Published by Mills Music Company.

Measures of Musical Ability, by Arnold Bentley. Published by George G. Harrap & Co. Ltd., London W.C.1, England.

Measures of Musical Talents, by Carl E. Seashore, Don Lewis, and Joseph G. Saetveit. Published by Psychological Corporation.

Musical Aptitude Profile, by Edwin Gordon. Published by Houghton Mifflin Company.

Musical Aptitude Test, by Harvey S. Whistler and Louis P. Thorpe. Published by California Test Bureau.

Test of Musicality, by E. Thayer Gaston. Published by Odell's Instrumental Service, Lawrence, Kansas.

Tilson-Gretsch Musical Aptitude Tests, by Lowell M. Tilson. Published by the Fred Gretsch Mfg. Co.

Wing Standardized Tests of Musical Intelligence, by Herbert Wing. Published by H. D. Wing and Cecilia Wing. Distributed by the National Foundation for Educational Research, London W1, England.

QUESTIONS FOR DISCUSSION

1. Point out similarities in content among the ten published measures of musical aptitude described in this chapter. Where different tests or test batteries purport to measure the same traits or abilities, point out differences in the form of the problems or of the answers required.

2. Point out similarities in content between the published measures and the unpublished tests described in this chapter. Where these similarities occur point out differences in procedure.

3. Point out the influences of early studies of musical aptitude mentioned in this chapter and earlier chapters upon both the published and the unpublished measures described here.

4. Consider the reliability and validity reports for the published tests. What should one consider in evaluating or comparing the coefficients provided in these reports?
5. Consider the information given concerning the reliability and validity studies reported for the Lundin tests. What implications may there be in this report for aptitude testing in music?
6. On the basis of the information provided in this chapter, evaluate and compare the published aptitude measures described here. Apply the evaluative criteria discussed in earlier chapters.
7. Describe any tests of musical aptitude or talent not listed in this chapter but with which you have had some experience or contact. Evaluate these tests according to criteria presented in previous chapters and by comparison with measures discussed here.

RECOMMENDED READINGS

Farnsworth, Paul R. *The Social Psychology of Music,* 2nd ed. Ames, Iowa: The Iowa State University Press, 1969. Chapter 9.

Lundin, Robert W. *An Objective Psychology of Music,* 2nd ed. New York: The Ronald Press Co., 1967. Chapter 13.

Schoen, Max. *Psychology of Music.* New York: The Ronald Press Co., 1940. Chapter 9.

Wing, Herbert. "Tests of Musical Ability and Appreciation." *British Journal of Psychology Monograph Supplements,* XXVII. London, England: Cambridge University Press, 1948.

CHAPTER 9

Measures of Achievement and Information

A number of tests designed to measure achievement in some type of musical endeavor or knowledge about music have been published over a period of about five decades. The majority of these have been concerned with knowledge of the rudiments of music. These attempt to measure the subject's knowledge of musical symbols and terms, key and meter signatures, interval structure, and similar rudiments of music theory. Some also measure the subject's ability to detect discrepancies in pitch or time between a musical example which he hears and one which he sees in notation. Some of the aptitude measures discussed in Chapter 8 also test this last ability and thus might, in this respect, be considered measures of achievement. Conversely, some consider this last type of test a measure of aptitude. The line is not always easy to draw.

Standardized achievement tests in music have, in general, attracted less attention and interest than have attempts at measuring aptitude for this field. There undoubtedly are a number of reasons for this. Most obvious, perhaps, is the fact that course content in various types of music activity is not very well standardized. Since achievement tests are linked closely to course content in most applications, teachers in general have found it preferable to construct their own measures of achievement. Too, perhaps because they seemed at first to promise solutions to problems more difficult for the individual teacher to solve by himself (e.g., prediction of success or failure), aptitude measures tended to overshadow the achievement tests in importance. Some teachers have objected to standardized measures of achievement, expressing the fear that their use leads to test-directed teaching. These critics feel that the result frequently is the inclusion of invalid, valueless material in course content. This, however, would seem to be the fault of the teacher and not of any tests used.

That some interest in achievement measures not only still exists but may be growing is evidenced by the appearance of several new measures of achievement within relatively recent years. Knowledge about such measures would seem to be an important part of the music teacher's equipment.

Beach. The earliest standardized measure of musical achievement to appear was the *Beach Music Test,* which was first published in 1920, revised in 1930, and reprinted in 1938. Written by Frank A. Beach and edited by H. E. Schrammel, the *Beach Music Test* consists of 11 parts, each of which attempts to measure a different aspect of knowledge about music.

Part One tests knowledge of musical symbols, including notes, rests, clefs, repeat marks, and major key signatures. Part Two tests the subject's feeling for metrical structure in music. The subject is asked to identify as duple, triple, or quadruple structure melodies which he hears. In one case the example is also written out, lacking meter signature and bar lines, which are to be supplied by the subject. Part Three is a test of "Tone Direction and Similarity." This includes recognition of ascending or descending direction of a melody and recognition of similarity between phrases or melodies.

Part Four is a test of pitch discrimination. The subject is required to identify by number the highest or lowest tone of a group. The six items include four two-note groups and two three-note groups. Part Five bears the title "Application of Syllables." In this section the subject identifies notes which he hears by syllable name. Thus this is a test of aural acuity and comprehension as well as of knowledge of syllable names.

Part Six tests knowledge of time values. The subject is required to identify visually the notes or rests which fall on specified beats of specified measures in a melody and to point out measures which contain too many or too few beats. Part Seven is a test of knowledge of musical terms and symbols. Ten items are included, covering tempo and dynamic markings, accent marks, accidentals, etc.

Part Eight is entitled, "Correction of Notation." This, in the main, is a measure of the ability to coordinate ear and eye. The subject is asked to pick from a number of written melodies that one which represents in notation the melody which he hears. In another question he is asked to point out discrepancies between melodies which he hears and those which appear on the answer form, and to identify the meter of one of the melodies. Another question presents in notation the first phrase of each of five songs, asking the subject to select from eight alternatives the titles of these songs. While the songs undoubtedly were well known at the time of publication of the *Beach Music Test,* some of them might not be familiar to those of a later generation.

Part Nine of the *Beach Music Test* tests knowledge of syllable and pitch names. The subject is asked to identify visually by syllable and by pitch name, notes which appear in notation. In Part Ten, entitled "Representation of Pitches," the subject is required to write on the staff the key signatures for two specified major keys. Both treble and bass clefs are used.

Part Eleven is a test of knowledge of composers and artists. The subject is required to match names of composers and artists with short identifying phrases. Most of the names included are those of composers whose importance probably is not significantly altered by the passage of time. Included also are names of a few artists who were well known to concert audiences at the time of publication of this test but whose names are far less familiar to concert audiences of our day. The list is completely lacking, of course, in names of composers who have achieved eminence during the past quarter of a century. These deficiencies, which are inevitable characteristics of a test of this type of knowledge, make questionable the value of this part of the test for current use.

With the exception of Part Eleven, which takes the form of matched columns, and of one or two questions in other parts which require the subject to write in key or meter signatures, the questions throughout are in the multiple choice form. Possible answers are numbered, and the subject places the number of his choice in the answer box provided.

Reliability coefficients, derived by the split-half method and averaging .86 for college students and .83 for high school students, have been reported for the *Beach Music Test*. The test has been validated against teacher rankings in (a) knowledge of musical fundamentals, and (b) general musicianship. The latter is not defined. Correlations with general musicianship range from .32 to .92 with a median of .65. Correlations between test scores and ratings of knowledge of musical fundamentals range from .14 to .94 with a median of .74. The test is provided with norms, and it is available from the Bureau of Educational Measurements of the State Teachers College at Emporia, Kansas.

Kwalwasser-Ruch. The *Kwalwasser-Ruch Test of Musical Accomplishment* actually is a set of ten tests covering knowledge of musical symbols and terms, knowledge of key and meter signatures, knowledge of note and rest values, recognition of syllable and pitch names, visual recognition of familiar melodies, and the ability to detect pitch and time errors in familiar melodies. It was designed by Jacob Kwalwasser and G. M. Ruch for use in grades 4 through 12. First published in 1924, the test was revised in 1927.

Test One is a test of knowledge of musical symbols and terms. Twenty-five items, covering dynamic markings, tempo and expression markings, accidentals, clefs, etc., are included. The subject underlines his choice among five possible answers for each item.

In Test Two, five items of six notes each are given in musical notation. The first note of each item is identified as "do," and the subject is required to write in the syllable name for each of the other notes. Both diatonic and chromatic notes are included.

In Test Three, the song "America" is presented in notation with several pitch errors (incorrect notes) included. The subject is asked to cross out all measures containing such errors. Test Four again presents "America" in notation, this time with several errors in note values. The subject again is asked to cross out those measures containing errors.

Test Five presents the subject with four items of six notes each. Two items are written in the treble clef two in the bass clef. In each item the first note is identified by letter name. The subject is required to write in the letter names for the remaining five notes in each section.

Test Six includes ten items, each consisting of a complete measure, but lacking a meter signature. From five possible answers for each item the subject is required to underline the meter signature which fits the measure given in notation.

Test Seven presents the subject with key signatures for ten major keys and five minor keys, all given on the treble staff. For each signature given, the subject is required to write in the name of the key.

Test Eight includes five items, each consisting of an incomplete measure. The subject is to select from five choices the single note which would correctly fill out the measure. Underlining again is the subject's method of indicating his choice. Test Nine is very similar to Test Eight. In this case each incomplete measure is to be completed with a rest.

Test Ten presents in musical notation a phrase from each of ten familiar songs. The subject is required to write in either the title of each song or the words of the text for each phrase.

The test manual gives detailed instructions for administration of the test, including time limits for each test of the set. Reliability coefficients, derived by the split-half method, range from .70 for Test Eight to .97 for Test One. The total score shows a reliability coefficient of .97, according to the test manual. Separate norms for each of grades 4 through 8 are included, and another set is given for grades 9 through 12. Norms are couched in deciles, and some explanation of their derivation is included in the manual. The Kwalwasser-Ruch test is published by the Bureau of Educational Research and Service of the State University of Iowa.

Providence Inventory. The *Providence Inventory Test in Music* by Richard D. Allen, Walter H. Butterfield, and Marguerite Tully, was copyrighted in 1932. Intended for use in grades 4 through 9, it is in ten parts, with a time limit placed upon each. According to the manual of directions, the entire test can be administered in 45 minutes. Separate norms, in percentiles, are provided for each grade level, and explicit instructions for administration of the test are provided in the manual.

Test One is a measure of the subject's ability to name notes written on the treble staff. The subject answers by printing the proper letter name under each of ten notes written on the staff.

Test Two measures the subject's ability to associate key signatures and major key centers in musical notation. Nine key signatures, written on the treble staff, are given and the subject is required to place on the staff beside each a whole note designating "do."

Test Three is a measure of knowledge of note symbol names. Four note symbols are printed and for each the subject is to choose from five possible answers (whole, half, quarter, etc.) the correct symbol name. The choice is indicated by underlining.

Test Four again concerns key signatures. Eleven key signatures are presented on the treble staff. The subject now is asked to print under each signature the name of the key for which that signature is used. In eight cases he is asked to name a major key; in three he is asked for a minor key.

Test Five requires the subject to name meter signatures for sample measures of notation. Each of the six items presents a complete measure, written on one pitch on the treble staff. The subject is asked to give the appropriate meter signature for each. It might be noted that in the instructions no value in beats is assigned to any note symbol. Consequently, there is some ambiguity involved. Should a measure consisting of one half note have a meter signature of $\frac{2}{4}$ or one of $\frac{4}{8}$; should one consisting of three half notes be considered to be in $\frac{3}{2}$ or in $\frac{6}{4}$? It undoubtedly was assumed by the test authors that the grouping of notes should provide an adequate guide in each case. Some teachers may question such an assumption.

Test Six involves the naming of rest symbols. The procedure is like that used in Test Three, with the subject underlining his choice among five possibilities. As in Test Three, four items are included.

Test Seven measures the subject's knowledge of syllable names. Six individual lines of music are presented in notation on the treble staff. A syllable name is printed under each note in each line, and the subject is informed that two syllable names in each line are incorrect. He is to cross out each of the incorrect syllable names.

Test Eight measures the ability to name melodies presented in notation. A phrase of each of seven melodies is given, and under each the subject is required to write the name of the melody. He is told to write the words of the phrase if he cannot think of the title.

Test Nine is another test of knowledge of syllable names, this time using the bass staff. Three individual lines of music are given, with syllable names under the notes. Three syllable names in each line are incorrect, and again the subject is to cross out these incorrect names.

Test Ten deals with the names of miscellaneous musical symbols. The nine items require the subject to name such symbols as sharps and flats, clefs, repeat marks, etc. In each case the subject must write in the appropriate name.

The test manual gives explicit instructions for administering the test and for scoring the answer papers, thus providing for uniformity in different situations. The *Providence Inventory Test in Music* is published by the World Book Company.

Strouse. The *Strouse Music Test,* devised by Catherine E. Strouse, was copyrighted in 1937 by the Bureau of Educational Measurements of the State Teachers College at Emporia, Kansas. Intended for grades 4 through 16, this test includes two divisions, each consisting of nine parts.

In the first division, Part I directs the subject to pick the highest note from each of three groups of notes which he hears. The choice is indicated by writing the number of the highest note in the space provided. In Part II the subject writes the number of the longest of the notes which he hears in each of two groups.

In Part III the subject is to indicate whether the melodies which he hears are in duple, triple, or quadruple meter. Two items are included. Part IV includes five items. In each "do" is given in notation in the treble clef, and before each item is played the subject is given the opportunity to sing the tonic arpeggio. Then he is to write on the staff each of the four tones which he hears in each item.

Part V calls for discrimination between melodies in major and minor modes. Three melodies are included, the subject underlining major or minor for each according to his decision.

Part VI tests the subject's ability to detect discrepancies between a melody which he hears and that given in notation. He is instructed to cross out on his paper the note which represents the deviation from the melody which he hears.

Part VII is a measure of retention. Each of the three items included contains a pair of exercises. If the two exercises are the same, a + mark is to be made in the space provided; if they are different, a − mark is the correct indication.

Part VIII is similar to Part VI. In the melody given in notation in this part, however, the subject is to cross out that measure which differs from the melody which he hears.

Part IX of the first division consists of a melody printed without bar lines. After hearing the melody twice, the subject is to supply the missing bar lines.

Part I of division two of the *Strouse Music Test* consists of 48 true-false questions covering musical terms and symbols, identification of composers with compositions, note values, etc. The subject is to place a + mark before each statement he believes to be true, a − mark before each one he believes false.

Part II of this division tests knowledge of key signatures. Three key signatures are given in notation on the treble staff. After each the subject is to place "do" and to write the letter name of the key in the blank provided.

Part III tests the subject's knowledge of names of lines and spaces of the staff. Ten notes are given in musical notation, five on the treble staff and five on the bass staff. Under each note symbol the subject is to write the correct letter name.

Part IV presents a melody in musical notation, but lacking a meter signature. The melody is divided into measures by bar lines. The subject is to provide the correct meter signature.

Part V reverses the question asked in Part IV. Here a melody is given in notation, with meter signature but lacking bar lines. The subject is to provide bar lines in accordance with the meter signature.

Part VI is a measure of association of syllable names with written note symbols. Each of the five items includes five notes written on the staff with key signatures. Four items use the treble staff, one the bass staff. Under each note symbol, the subject is to place the syllable name associated with that note of the key. Both diatonic and chromatic notes are included.

Part VII of division two is concerned with minor scales. Three minor scales are given in notation. Under each the subject is to write the name of the key and the form of the minor scale used.

Part VIII consists of 20 multiple choice items testing knowledge of instruments, various musical terms and symbols, etc. Part IX tests the subject's ability to recognize familiar songs in notation. The question is given in the form of two columns to be matched. Brief sections of five melodies are given in notation, to be matched with their correct titles, chosen from 12 possibilities listed. As in the *Beach Music Test,* some of the songs used might justifiably be unfamiliar to a more recent generation of subjects.

The *Strouse Music Test* is provided with percentile norms at the various grade levels. As with all measures of achievement the value of this test depends largely upon how closely its content corresponds with the content of the course or activity in which achievement is to be measured. Some teachers may question the curricular value of some of the knowledge which this test seeks to measure, and the validity and significance of some of the material included are equally questionable.

Kotick-Torgerson. A more recent addition to the list of measures of musical achievement is the *Diagnostic Tests of Achievement in Music* by M. Lila Kotick and T. L. Torgerson. This set of tests was published in 1950 by the California Test Bureau.

The set includes ten tests covering those aspects of musical theory commonly referred to as rudiments of music. Test 1 measures the subject's ability to associate syllable names with written note symbols. Eight groups of five notes each are written on the treble staff, each group having a different key signature. The subject is to give the syllable name of each note, selecting one answer from five choices given.

Test 2 is similar to Test 1 in that it measures ability to associate syllable names with written notes. Whereas in Test 1 only diatonic notes are used, Test 2 presents only chromatic notes. Test 2 consists of four items, each including five notes, and again the multiple choice form of answer is used.

Test 3 measures ability to associate number names of scale tones with written note symbols. Five items, each consisting of five notes, are included, and the procedure is the same as that used in Tests 1 and 2. The subject selects the correct number name for each note from five choices presented.

Test 4 is a measure of knowledge of meter signatures or, to use the terminology of the test instructions, time signatures. Ten meter signatures are presented, and the subject is asked how many beats per measure are indicated by each of the signatures. Again the subject selects his answer from five choices given. It might be of interest to some teachers that under the $\frac{6}{8}$ signature both two beats and six beats are included among the choices, and under $\frac{9}{8}$ both three beats and nine beats are included.

Test 5 is concerned with visual distinction between major and minor modes. Each of the ten items included consists of two measures of musical notation which, the subject is told, represent the two final measures of a melody. The subject is to indicate whether the melody is in the major or the minor mode.

Test 6 of the *Diagnostic Tests of Achievement in Music* measures knowledge of values of note and rest symbols. Under each of 20 note and rest symbols given with meter signature, the subject is to indicate the value in terms of beats. Again five choices are offered for each answer.

Test 7 tests knowledge of letter names. Four items are included, each consisting of five notes printed on the treble staff or on leger lines above or below the treble staff. From the five choices given below each note, the subject is to select the correct name of that note.

Test 8 concerns knowledge of names of various musical symbols. The 20 items cover various note and rest symbols, key and meter signatures, dynamic markings, accidentals, and the like. The subject selects the answer from ten choices.

Test 9 requires the subject to associate key names with signatures. Each of the ten items consists of a key signature written on the treble staff. Under each the subject is to select from ten choices the proper key name. Since the same ten choices are offered under every key signature, the actual number of choices decreases with each answer made. Presumably only major keys are involved, although no such direction is included either on the test blank or in the instructions. The list of choices for all but two of the signatures includes the names of both major and minor keys using that signature.

Test 10, the final section of this set, is a measure of song recognition. Each of the 20 items consists of a segment of a familiar melody, given in musical notation on a separate sheet. From the five choices accompanying each melodic fragment, the subject is to select the correct title.

The answer sheet provided is an IBM sheet which can be scored by machine or by stencil. The subject indicates each of his answers by filling in the space between two parallel dotted lines, the usual procedure with machine scoring sheets.

The test manual is complete with detailed instructions for administration and scoring. No real norms are provided since the authors believe that such norms would have little meaning due to diversity of curricula in music, inconsistency in grade placement of topics, and differing emphases in course content in different schools. Instead of giving norms the authors suggest a per cent system of evaluation, with each teacher or school setting its own standard of mastery. This seems an unsatisfactory substitute for norms.

Reliability coefficients, computed by the Kuder-Richardson formula, are given for each of the sub-tests and for total score. Coefficients for the separate tests, based on data for grades 4 through 10, range from .51 to .93 with a median of .90. Coefficients given for each grade level on the total score, derived from the data for the seven grade levels is .97.

Time limits for each test are suggested in the manual, but it is emphasized that these limits should not be rigidly adhered to.

Knuth. The *Knuth Achievement Tests in Music,* published in 1936, are designed to measure only association of melodies heard with those seen in notation. Two forms of the tests are available, and the set is designed for use at three levels, grades 3 and 4, grades 5 and 6, and grades 7 through 12.

The test consists of forty items. Each is a four-measure melody, played on the piano. On the test blank each melody is presented in notation. The first two measures of the melody always appear as played, with four alternative versions of the last two measures given. From the four versions the student selects the one which he hears by marking a cross in the proper blank. Each melody is played once, preceded by the sounding of the tonic chord.

The test author reports reliability coefficients of .81, .81, and .84, respectively, for the three levels of the tests. These coefficients were derived through the parallel forms method. A coefficient of .96 was derived for the three levels combined, using the split half method with 239 college freshmen. Content validity is assumed on the basis of judgments of six music educators and an analysis of nine school music series of the time. Truncated tables of percentile norms are given separately for each level of the tests and at the high school level for subjects in various musical performing areas.

Originally designed for administration from the piano and published by the Educational Test Bureau, the *Knuth Achievement Tests in Music* now are available on tapes and film strips from Creative Arts Research Associates.

Snyder Knuth. The *Snyder Knuth Music Achievement Test* by Alice Snyder Knuth was copyrighted in 1968 by Creative Arts Research Associates, Inc. Designed to measure understanding of musical notation, the test is in four parts entitled Listening and Seeing, Listening, Music Comprehension, and Tonal Memory. Two parallel forms are available.

Part I, Listening and Seeing, is in large part similar to the older *Knuth Achievement Tests in Music* in that it tests the subject's ability to associate with music notation melodic patterns which he hears. In each item a short melodic pattern is played on the piano and presented in notation, with four written alternatives for part of the pattern. The subject selects from the four written alternatives that which, in his opinion, is the correct notation of what is played. The last few items of Part I are completely different in nature. In each of these the subject is asked to select from four choices a chord progression (I IV V I, etc.) which provides the best simple harmonization (one chord per measure) for the melody which is presented in notation. The choice is made entirely on a visual basis. Part I includes a total of fifty-three items.

Part II, Listening, contains thirty-eight items which test the subject's auditory abilities in several different ways. In each of the first few items the subject is asked to select from four alternative line contours the one which would best describe the melodic contour of the musical phrase played on the piano. Several items ask the subject to count the number of times the key tone appears in a melodic pattern which he hears. Similarly, in some items the subject is asked to count the number of times the tonic chord appears and in others the number of octave intervals included. Other items in Part II require the subject to identify aurally phrases of a melody which are alike or almost alike, to indicate whether a melody "swings" in two's or three's, and to determine whether a melody is in the major or minor mode.

Part III of the *Snyder Knuth Music Achievement Test* tests the subject's knowledge of elements of musical notation (clefs, repeat signs, etc.), chord structures, syllable names, etc., through analogies. In each item two elements are presented to establish a relationship, and from four choices the subject is asked to select a set of two elements which are in a similar relationship. In other items of this part the subject is expected to associate rhythmic backgrounds with types of bodily movement such as walking, running, and skipping. All of Part III is done visually.

Part IV also is entirely visual. In each item a phrase of a well known melody is presented in musical notation and the subject is asked to identify the melody from four choices.

Aural aspects of the *Snyder Knuth Music Achievement Test* are recorded on tape and instructions are given orally on the tapes. Each item is announced by number on the tapes, including those items for which there is no auditory stimulus. Visual aspects are presented on film strips. The subject responds to the test items by marking appropriate spaces on an answer sheet which can be scored by machine or by hand with the aid of a scoring stencil.

The test manual is a seven page pamphlet which gives directions for administration and scoring of the test, suggestions for use of test results, information on reliability and validity, and norms for college majors in elementary education. The test author derived a reliability coefficient of .993 using the parallel forms method with 311 elementary education students at the college level, and one of .998 using the same method with 64 advanced college music majors. Content validity is claimed in a brief statement which cites as a basis courses of study, textbooks, and curriculum guides prepared for elementary teachers and for the preparation of elementary teachers. Norms are given only for college majors in elementary education, and for these only in an incomplete table of percentile norms, although the manual suggests that the test may also be used with music majors at both college and secondary levels and at the elementary level.

The information given in the manual is brief and rather cursory in nature. More information about the development of the test and additional data on reliability and validity would be desirable, and it is to be hoped that additional studies of the test will yield the latter. The tapes are adequate for the purpose although the quality of the piano tone is disappointing, and a few rather sudden and marked changes in loudness in the instructions are disconcerting. These should not affect the validity of the testing, however, if warning is given.

Since relatively little information about the *Snyder Knuth Music Achievement Test* is available, it is difficult to evaluate at this time. It should be of interest, however, to those concerned with the instruction in music of college elementary education majors, and studies of its effectiveness should be encouraged.

Jones. The *Jones Music Recognition Test* by Archie N. Jones was published in 1949 by Carl Fischer, Inc. The test is divided into two levels, Part 1 for grades 4-8 and Part 2 for grades 9-16.

Part 1 consists of 80 items played in groups of ten. Each item is an excerpt from a musical composition and the subject is asked to identify each excerpt in a group from a list of twelve titles.

Part 2 is similar but the subject is asked to identify also the composers of the compositions from which excerpts are played. There are 100 items in this part of the test.

The test is administered from the piano. The author has provided no data on reliability or validity, but Wing[1], using a tape recorded presentation with 150 college students, found a split half reliability coefficient of .76 for Part 2.

Like any test which depends upon specific musical literature the *Jones Music Recognition Test* probably has become dated. Some of the compositions which one might have expected students to know in 1949 may be unfamiliar to a later generation.

Aliferis. The *Aliferis Music Achievement Test-College Entrance Level,* first copyrighted in 1947, is designed to measure auditory-visual discrimination of melodic, harmonic, and rhythmic elements and idioms.

The Aliferis test is in three sections, each with two parts. The first section deals with recognition of melodic elements and idioms in music. In part one the subject is presented with four musical intervals in notation. He is to select one of the four as the interval which he hears played on the piano. In part two the subject hears a four note melodic pattern which he is to match with one of four choices given in notation. The variable actually is the final note of the pattern.

Section two of the test is concerned with harmonic elements and idioms. In the first part of this section the subject hears a four-voiced arrangement of a chord played twice at the piano with a brief pause between soundings. From four choices given in notation he is to select the chord which he has heard. In part two a three chord sequence is played twice, with a brief pause between playings. This time the subject selects his answer from three possibilities.

In section three of the test, identification of rhythmic elements and idioms is measured. The test author defines a rhythmic ele-

---

[1]Oscar K. Buros, *Sixth Mental Measurements Yearbook.* Highland Park, N. J.: Gryphon Press, 1964. p. 622.

ment as a rhythmic figure of one beat duration. The example played in each case consists of a C major scale built of three successive presentations of the same one beat rhythmic figure. The subject selects from four choices the rhythmic element from which the scale is built. Part two is similar in its general nature. Here, rhythmic idioms, each of which consists of a combination of two rhythmic elements, are presented. Again the subject selects his answer from four choices.

Sixty-four items are included in the test. Section one contains 26, section two contains 18, and section three has 20. Reliability coefficients have been calculated for the separate sections as well as for the totaled score. Those for the separate sections are .84, .72, and .67. The coefficient for the totaled score is .88.

Validity of the *Aliferis Music Achievement Test-College Entrance Level* for the purpose of predicting success in college level music theory courses was investigated by Roby.[2] Using grades in music theory earned by seventy-seven students in a two year course sequence as a validating criterion Roby found coefficients of .728, .643, .662, and .373, respectively, for the total test, the melody test, the harmony test, and the rhythm test. These coefficients, with the exception of that for the rhythm test, were very significantly greater than those found in the same study for the *Minnesota English Entrance Test* and the *American Council on Education Psychological Examination* and theory grades. Comparable coefficients for the Seashore Measures were negligible. The small number of subjects (77) involved in the study makes its results less than conclusive, but it does provide an indication that the *Aliferis Music Achievement Test* does possess satisfactory validity for the prognostication of success in college music theory courses of traditional content.

The *Aliferis Music Achievement Test-College Entrance Level* appears to be the result of sound and exhaustive scientific procedures. Detailed instructions for the administration of the test are given in the manual, and it is relatively easy to score. Both geographical and national norms, based on some 1,700 cases, are provided. The test can be administered from the piano, but

---

[2]A. Richard Roby, "A Study in the Correlation of Music Theory Grades With the Seashore Measures of Musical Talents and the Aliferis Music Achievement Test," *Journal of Research in Music Education*, X, 2 (Fall, 1962).

it also is available on a pre-recorded tape. The latter is to be preferred, of course, in the interest of standardization.

Aliferis-Stecklein. The *Aliferis-Stecklein Music Achievement Test— College Midpoint Level* was formulated to provide a standardized measure of auditory-visual discrimination after two years of study in college music theory courses. Like its predecessor, the *Aliferis Music Achievement Test—College Entrance Level,* the Aliferis-Stecklein test consists of three sections dealing with auditory-visual discrimination in its melodic, harmonic, and rhythmic aspects.

Section one—Melodic Interval Test—presents the subject with thirty- four items, each of which consists of four tones played melodically on the piano. In each item the subject is asked to identify from four choices the fourth tone of the pattern. Both the first three tones of the pattern and the four alternative final tones appear in notation on the test blank.

The Chord Test, which comprises the second section of the *Aliferis-Stecklein Music Achievement Test,* consists of twenty-six items, each of which presents a four-voice chord played harmonically on the piano. The subject is to compare the chord which is played with the chord which appears in notation on the test blank. One tone is always different and the subject is to identify the voice in which the discrepancy occurs. The voices are clearly marked with the appropriate letters in the test booklet.

Section three, the Rhythm Test, includes nineteen items. Each consists of a six-beat rhythmic pattern played melodically on the piano. The rhythm of each pattern appears in notation on the test sheet. In one beat of each pattern there is a rhythmic discrepancy between the pattern played and that which appears in notation. The subject is to identify the beat in which the discrepancy occurs by writing in the letter associated with it on the test blank.

The *Aliferis-Stecklein Music Achievement Test—College Midpoint Level* is available on tape or it may be administered from the piano. The tape includes examples and test items but instructions must be read by the test administrator both when the test is given by tape and from the piano. Again, to avoid differences in style of presentation of items, use of the taped version is recommended.

The test manual provides a history of the development of the test, information on item difficulty and item discrimination as well as reliability and validity, and detailed instructions for administration of the test and interpretation of scores. Norms are provided in standard scores and percentile ranks.

Using a Kuder-Richardson formula the authors derived reliability coefficients of .90, .84, .69, and .92, respectively, for the Melodic Interval Test, the Chord Test, the Rhythm Test, and the total score. Validity was studied by correlating totaled test scores with honor point averages attained in their first two years by 206 music students, both in music courses and in all courses. Coefficients of .44 and .42, respectively, were found.

Like that of the college entrance level test, the development of the Aliferis-Stecklein test seems to have been careful and thorough. One reviewer, Herbert Wing, has found it disappointing as compared with the Aliferis college entrance level test. He questions its discriminating power and suggests that the interpretation in the manual of reliability and validity statistics may be overly optimistic.[3]

Both the *Aliferis Music Achievement Test—College Entrance Level* and the *Aliferis-Stecklein Music Achievement Test—College Midpoint Level* are published by the University of Minnesota Press.

Kwalwasser. The *Kwalwasser Test of Music Information and Appreciation* by Jacob Kwalwasser was copyrighted in 1927 by the Bureau of Educational Research and Service of the University of Iowa. Designed for use in high schools and colleges, the test is in nine parts which seek to measure (1) knowledge of artists by performing medium, (2) knowledge of composers by nationality, (3) knowledge of compositions by composer, (4) knowledge of composers by the types of composition for which they were best known, (5) general knowledge of composers and compositions, (6) knowledge of orchestral instruments by type of sound stimulus, (7) knowledge of orchestral instruments by orchestral choir, (8) general knowledge of instrumentation, and (9) general knowledge of music structure and form.

---

[3]Oscar K. Buros, *Sixth Mental Measurements Yearbook*. Highland Park, N. J.: Gryphon Press, 1964. p. 621.

While some parts of the test are as valid as they were at the time of publication, others are outdated as are all tests which deal with artists and compositions well known in a bygone period but of less importance to later generations. The significance of some of the information sought also is questionable, although it undoubtedly was included in many high school music appreciation courses of the nineteen twenties. More valid measures of musical knowledge are available or can be made up for present day use.

Colwell. The *Music Achievement Tests* by Richard Colwell are a recent and important contribution to achievement testing in music. As originally published in 1968 by the Follett Educational Corporation the battery included two tests, each of which is subdivided into several parts.

Test 1 includes three parts, concerned respectively with pitch discrimination, interval discrimination, and meter discrimination. Part 1, Pitch Discrimination, is further divided into two subtests. Subtest A consists of fifteen items, each of which presents two tones played by a violin or a 'cello. The test subject is asked to tell which tone is higher if they are different, or to tell if they are the same. The smallest pitch difference used is the semitone and the items are played at widely varying pitch levels. Subtest B includes ten items, each of which presents three tones. The subject is asked to identify by number the lowest of the three tones.

Part 2 of Test 1 attempts to measure interval discrimination through two subtests. Subtest A consists of ten items, each of which presents a pattern of three tones. The subject is asked to indicate whether the tones move scalewise or by leap. He also may so indicate if he is in doubt, providing a three option answer. Again a violin and a 'cello are the performing media, presenting the items at different pitch levels. Subtest B presents phrases taken from folk and art songs. In each case the subject is asked to indicate whether the tonal movement in the phrase is generally scalewise or by leap. Again a third option is provided by allowing the expression of doubt.

Part 3, Meter Discrimination, includes fifteen items each of which consists of a phrase taken from a song. The items are played on a piano, with harmonic accompaniment. The subject is asked to indicate whether the phrase is in duple or triple meter or if he is in doubt.

Test 2 also has three parts, concerned respectively with major-minor mode discrimination, feeling for tonal center, and auditory-visual discrimination. Each part is further divided into two subtests.

Part 1, Subtest A, consists of fifteen items each of which presents two chords played on a piano. Both chords in an item are either major or minor, and the subject is asked to indicate which mode the two chords are in. Subtest B presents phrases of songs commonly found in elementary music books, played on the piano with appropriate harmony. Each phrase may be entirely in the major mode, entirely in the minor mode, or may change from one to the other. The subject is asked to indicate in each case whether the phrase is in the major mode, in the minor mode, or changes from one to the other.

Part 2 attempts to measure feeling for tonal center. Subtest A requires the subject to determine the key center of a group of chords. Each of the ten items presents a four chord progression, culminating in the tonic chord with the tonic note in both soprano and bass. The chord progression is followed by three single tones, and the subject is asked to identify by number which of the three is the tonic note. He also may indicate that none of the three is the tonic note. Subtest B is similar in its nature and demands, but harmonized musical phrases are used instead of simple chord progressions. Again, in each item three single tones are presented immediately after the phrase, and the subject is asked to indicate which, if any, of the three is the tonic note. If none of the three is the tonic, the subject may so indicate, thus having a choice of four responses.

Part 3 of Test 2 seeks to measure auditory-visual discrimination. Subtest A asks the test subject to identify every measure of a four measure phrase in which there is a pitch discrepancy between what he hears and what he sees in notation. He is asked only to indicate where a discrepancy occurs, not the form of the discrepancy. Subtest B is very similar, but in this case the subject is required to detect discrepancies in rhythm rather than in pitch.

Two more tests were added to the *Music Achievement Test* battery and published by the Follett Educational Corporation in 1970. Test 3 contains four parts. Part 1, Tonal Memory, presents in each of its items a chord played harmonically followed by basically the same chord played in arpeggio form. The subject is asked to tell which note of the arpeggio is changed from the composition of the block chord or if none is different. Since there are four tones in each chord and arpeggio, the subject has a choice of five responses for each item. The piano is used to present the chords.

Each item of Part 2, Melody Recognition, presents a melody played first alone on the piano, followed by the same melody played in a three-voice harmonic context by a string trio. The subject is asked to indicate whether, in the harmonic version, the melody is in the high, middle, or low voice. He also may indicate doubt, thus having four response options in each item.

Part 3, Pitch Recognition, measures the subject's ability to hear tones in relation to one another. The subject first hears and sees in notation a standard or reference note. He then sees in notation a second note and hears three choices from which he is to pick none or one as that which is represented by the written note.

Part 4 attempts to test aural recognition of instruments. In each of the ten items of Subtest A a short musical selection is played unaccompanied, and the subject is expected to identify the performing instrument from four choices or to indicate that it is none of these. In the five items of Subtest B the principal musical line is presented in an orchestral context and may be played by a single instrument or several of the same kind. The subject again may identify the instrument playing the principal line from four alternate answers or may indicate that none of these is correct. Because of the small number of items in this test it is not scored separately.

Test 4 also contains four parts. Part 1, Musical Style, is further divided into two subtests. Subtest A asks the test subject to identify from four choices the composer whose style is most like that of the musical excerpt played in each item. Subtest B asks the subject to characterize the texture of each short musical selection played as monophonic, homophonic, or polyphonic. As a fourth alternative the subject may indicate his doubt.

Part 2 of Test 4 is another measure of audio-visual discrimination. As in Subtest B of Part 3, Test 2, the subject is required to identify by number each measure in a four-measure selection in which there is a rhythmic discrepancy between what is played and what appears in notation. Any, all, or none of the four measures may contain a discrepancy. According to the test author this test is more difficult than the audio-visual rhythmic discrimination subtest in Test 2.

Part 3 is a measure of chord recognition. In each of the fifteen items the subject is asked to identify which, if any, of three comparison chords is the same as the chord played as a standard. He also may indicate doubt, thus choosing from four possible answers.

Part 4 calls for recognition of cadences. In each of the fifteen items a short phrase is played, and the subject is asked to indicate whether the cadence is a full cadence, a half cadence, or a deceptive cadence, or to indicate his doubt.

Each of the tests of the *Music Achievement Tests* by Colwell is contained on a twelve-inch long-playing record. Instructions to the subject and examples are included on the record, and the number of each test item is announced. The records are of good quality in both performance and technical aspects. An *Administrative and Scoring Manual*, which includes some norms as well as explicit instructions for administering and scoring the test, is available for each of the tests in the battery.

In addition to the individual *Administrative and Scoring Manuals* for the four tests of the battery, two *Interpretive Manuals* are available—one for Tests 1 and 2 and the other for Tests 3 and 4. These manuals include extensive material on reliability of the tests, norms, and explanations of the development of the battery as well as instructions for administration and scoring. Reliability coefficients for Tests 1 and 2 are given by grade levels, four through high school, for total scores and for individual tests and subtests as determined by a Kuder-Richardson formula. Those for total scores range from .797 to .965 with most in the upper .80's and the .90's, and those for part scores from .425 to .866.

Reliability coefficients for Tests 3 and 4 are given by grade levels, four through twelve and five through twelve, and by various kinds of groupings for total and part scores, again as determined by a Kuder-Richardson formula. Coefficients for total scores on Test 3 range from .460 to .907 with most in the .80's, and those for part scores range from .382 to .803. For Test 4 coefficients for total scores range from .814 to .883, and those for part scores from .254 to .809 with the majority in the .70's and .80's.

Norms also are provided in the *Interpretive Manuals* for total scores and for part scores for various kinds of groupings of subjects, from Grade 4 through Grade 12 for Tests 1, 2, and 3 and from Grade 5 through Grade 12 for Test 4.

Answers are indicated by filling in blanks on the answer sheets, and the tests may be scored by hand or by machine. Instructions are given for both methods.

The *Music Achievement Tests* were designed by their author to provide a measure of achievement of some important objectives of school music programs. Important objectives were identified through (1) an examination of elementary music series published by leading houses; (2) an inspection of curriculum guides, courses of study, and texts on elementary music used in college courses; (3) an analysis of *The Study of Music in the Elementary School—A Conceptual Approach* and *Music in General Education,* published by the Music Educators National Conference; (4) an examination of texts on the psychology of music; and (5) a conference of authorities on school music. Content validity of the *Music Achievement Tests* is assumed on the basis of these five steps.

Perhaps the outstanding feature of the *Music Achievement Tests* is that they emphasize the auditory aspect of music. Too many earlier attempts at standardized measures of musical achievement emphasized knowledge of notation and other facts *about* music at the expense of aural perception. Colwell has made a very interesting contribution to the literature of music tests, and it is to be hoped that research studies and use of the battery will provide more information about its advantageous utilization.

Farnum. Another measure of auditory-visual discrimination which has appeared in relatively recent years is the *Farnum Music No-*

tation Test by Stephen E. Farnum. This test was published in 1953 by The Psychological Corporation of New York City.

The test consists of 40 four-measure melodic phrases. One measure of each melody played is different from the accompanying melody in notation. The differences may be in pitch, in rhythm, or in both. In reality, more than 75 per cent of the changes are in pitch. The subject answers by indicating the number of the measure in which the change has been made.

The *Farnum Music Notation Test* was designed for use in grades 7 through 9. Reliability coefficients, derived by the split-half technique, are reported separately for boys and girls and these range from .78 to .91. A reliability coefficient, computed by the Kuder-Richardson formula, also has been reported by Bentley.[4] This coefficient, which was derived from data obtained from about two hundred high school students, was .892. The same investigator, using the Farnum test in a comparative study of several musical aptitude tests, obtained a correlation of .495 between scores on this test and grades in music courses.[5] Larson,[6] reviewing the test in the *Fifth Mental Measurements Yearbook*, has expressed the view that this test actually measures an ability which is symptomatic of musical aptitude—a view which would seem to be implicit in its use in the Bentley study.

Percentile norms are given separately for boys and girls, and also for students who have had special instruction and those who have not. Norms for the total group also are included. The test is available on one 78 r.p.m. record, which includes both instructions and item numbers.

Other Early Measures. Among the earlier published measures of musical achievement or knowledge were the *Musical Achievement Test* by Gildersleeve, the *Kelsey Standardized Tests of Musical Achievement*, the *Torgerson-Fahnestock Music Test*, the *McCauley Experiment in Public School Music*, and the *Hutchinson Music*

---

[4]R. R. Bentley, "A Critical Comparison of Certain Music Aptitude Tests." Doctoral Dissertation, published on microfilm, University of Southern California, 1955. p. 271.

[5]Ibid., p. 301.

[6]Oscar K. Buros, *Fifth Mental Measurements Yearbook*. Highland Park, N. J.: Gryphon Press, 1959. p. 382.

Tests. The first four of these cover the same general areas tested by several of the measures already described. The Gildersleeve *Musical Achievement Test* measures knowledge of musical symbols, musical instruments, musical terms, types of compositions, famous names, and familiar melodies. The Kelsey tests deal with the general fundamentals of music, with a very small sampling of eminent names of the time. The *Torgerson-Fahnestock Music Test* delves into knowledge of musical symbols, key and meter signatures, pitch and syllable names, minor scales, and the like. It also tests aural perception through dictated tests concerned with pitch and time errors, meter signatures, and syllable names. The *McCauley Experiment in Public School Music* covers the same material in general as the Gildersleeve test. It is much longer than the former, however, taking about an hour and a half to administer. The Hutchinson tests deal only with visual recognition of familiar tunes. Groups of phrases from tunes well known in the 1920's are presented, together with lists of titles from which the subject is to choose the proper one for each phrase. Since these five tests are infrequently used and are not distinguished by unusual features, there seems to be no need to discuss them in further detail.

Watkins-Farnum. An attempt to measure a different kind of achievement in music—actual musical performance—has resulted from the work of John Watkins and Stephen E. Farnum. This is the *Watkins-Farnum Performance Scale for All Band Instruments,* available from Hal Leonard Music, Incorporated, of Winona, Minnesota.

This test consists of 14 sight-reading exercises which are graded in difficulty. An objective system of scoring has been worked out on the basis of pitch and rhythmic accuracy, observation of tempo and expression markings, observation of slur markings, and observation of repeat signs. The test booklet provides explicit instructions for administration and scoring. It also provides a summary of construction procedures and information on reliability and validity. Reliability coefficients, obtained by the equivalent forms method for three grade levels, are .87, .94, and .94. Coefficients for correlations between test scores and teacher rankings of students range from .68 to .87 with a median of .83. The groups used to provide the data for these correlations were rather small.

Objective measurement of musical performance is a highly desirable goal. The *Watkins-Farnum Performance Scale* represents a limited measure of performance as any such test probably must, since certain aspects of performance do not seem to be susceptible to objective measurement. The Scale appears to have been worked out with considerable care, however, and it seems to be based upon scientific principles of measurement insofar as any measure of performance can be. It was copyrighted in 1954.

Early Performance Tests. Measures of vocal performance had been produced in earlier years by E. K. Hillbrand, R. M. Mosher, and A. W. Otterstein and Mosher. The earliest of these was the *Hillbrand Sight Singing Test,* published in 1923 by the World Book Company. Designed for pupils in grades 4 through 6, the test presents six songs which the test subject sings, after a few moments for study, without help or accompaniment. The performance then is scored on the basis of intonation, wrong notes, notes omitted, notes added, errors in time, and repetitions and hesitations.

The *Mosher Test of Individual Singing* was published in 1925 by the Bureau of Publications of Columbia Teachers College. This test includes 12 items arranged in order of difficulty. These items are presented to the test subject and then sung back by him. The score is based on the number of measures sung correctly in pitch and rhythm.

Mosher also collaborated with A. W. Otterstein to produce the *O-M Sight Singing Test,* published by the Stanford University Press in 1932. In structure this test is much like the earlier one by Mosher. The 28 exercises use both major and minor modes, and some of the more difficult ones begin on scale steps other than the tonic. Specific instructions are given for marking and evaluating the subject's performance of these exercises.

All of these performance scales are, of course, individual tests. The nature of musical performance, obviously, makes group measurement impossible.

SUMMARY

A significant number of measures of musical achievement have been published during the four decades beginning in 1920. Most of them have been tests of knowledge of rudiments of music theory, although a number of them have also attempted to measure auditory-visual discrimination—the ability to associate what is heard with what is seen in notation. A few authors have presented scales which attempt to objectify the evaluation of musical performance.

The value of any achievement test in any situation depends largely upon how well the content of the test corresponds with what is to be measured in that situation, i.e., the curricular validity of the test. Reliability, as always, is a prerequisite for validity.

Standardized measures of achievement have excited less interest in general than have measures of musical aptitude. Several reasons undoubtedly account for this. Such measures, however, may be of great aid to the music teacher in some situations. Knowledge about them would seem to be an important part of the teacher's equipment.

MUSICAL ACHIEVEMENT MEASURES DESCRIBED IN THIS CHAPTER

Aliferis Music Achievement Test—College Entrance Level, by James Aliferis. Published by the University of Minnesota Press.

Aliferis-Stecklein Music Achievement Test—College Midpoint Level, by James Aliferis and John E. Stecklein. Published by the University of Minnesota Press.

Beach Music Test, by Frank A. Beach. Published by the Bureau of Educational Measurements, Kansas State Teachers College, Emporia, Kansas.

Diagnostic Tests of Achievement in Music, by M. Lola Kotick and T. L. Torgerson. Published by California Test Bureau.

Farnum Music Notation Test, by Stephen E. Farnum. Published by Psychological Corporation.

Jones Music Recognition Test, by Archie N. Jones. Published by Carl Fischer, Inc.

Knuth Achievement Tests in Music, by William E. Knuth. Published by Creative Arts Research Associates.

Kwalwasser Test of Music Information and Appreciation, by Jacob Kwalwasser. Published by the Bureau of Educational Research and Service, University of Iowa.

Kwalwasser-Ruch Test of Musical Accomplishment, by Jacob
Kwalwasser and G. M. Ruch. Published by the Bureau of
Educational Research and Service, University of Iowa.

Music Achievement Tests, by Richard Colwell. Published by Follett Educational Corporation.

Providence Inventory Test in Music, by Richard D. Allen, Walter
H. Butterfield, and Marguerite Tully. Published by World
Book Company.

Snyder Knuth Music Achievement Test, by Alice Snyder Knuth.
Published by Creative Arts Research Associates.

Strouse Music Test, by Catherine E. Strouse. Published by the
Bureau of Educational Measurements, Kansas State Teachers
College, Emporia, Kansas.

Watkins-Farnum Performance Scale for All Band Instruments, by
John Watkins and Stephen E. Farnum. Published by Hal Leonard Music, Inc., Winona, Minnesota.

QUESTIONS FOR DISCUSSION

1. Compare the published measures of achievement described in
this chapter in order to detect common content areas. Which
ones attempt to measure the same areas of achievement or
knowledge? How do these differ in procedure?
2. How might a standardized measure of achievement be of help
in your teaching situation? What type of test would be of
greatest help?
3. What dangers might be inherent in the use of an objective
measure of musical performance? What aspects of performance
probably are not susceptible to objective measurement? How
might such measures be used intelligently?
4. What factors should one consider in evaluating any achievement test for use in any situation?

RECOMMENDED READING

Farnsworth, Paul R. *The Social Psychology of Music,* 2nd ed. Ames,
Iowa: The Iowa State University Press, 1969.

CHAPTER 10

Classroom Tests and Course Grading

Teachers of music in many schools, especially at the secondary and college levels, have the same need for proficiency in the construction of classroom tests and in determining course grades as teachers in other areas. While in some types of music teaching situations, e.g., instrumental music in the elementary school, some teachers may not be required to grade their students, in a greater number the teacher must meet such a requirement. Teachers of music courses in the high school usually must grade their students periodically, and in many schools grades are given in band, orchestra, chorus, and other group performance courses or activities. In the college, of course, the teacher of music courses must submit grades periodically just as instructors of other courses do. The need for measurement for purposes of diagnosing student weaknesses and of evaluating both student progress and teaching effectiveness also is present in music as in other fields. Effective techniques of measurement and evaluation, therefore, are as important to the music teacher as to his colleagues in other subject areas.

The general problems encountered by music teachers in devising and scoring classroom tests and in determining course grades are much the same as those met by teachers of other subjects. The number and extent of the difficulties involved very frequently depend upon the nature of the material or content of the course. Certain types of course material lend themselves quite well to objective measurement, while other types seem less well suited to the use of objective tests. Some kinds of course material do not permit the use of such measures at all.

Music teachers in general undoubtedly are as unsystematic in their grading practices as teachers in any area, and very likely more so than most. This probably is due in large part to the fact that so many aspects of music, and consequently music education, are so difficult to approach through objective means. Only limited aspects of musical performance, for example, can be measured, and questions remain as to the value of such measurement to the general appraisal of the totality of a performance. Important outcomes of other avenues of music study appear to the teacher to be virtually impossible to measure by objective methods. In the face of these difficulties, it may be that many music teachers are too ready to admit defeat in attempts to develop more systematic grading procedures.

Similar difficulties confront teachers in other areas. Actual performance is difficult to measure in many fields, and important course objectives in a number of other areas seem as intangible as those in music. As long as grades are required in music, valid techniques of measurement and evaluation are as essential to the music teacher as to his colleagues in other disciplines.

It would seem to many that the principal, if not the sole, requisite for valid measurement and evaluation in any field is a thorough knowledge of the subject matter involved. A teacher with a thorough knowledge of history, according to this belief, should be well equipped to measure the attainments of students in a history course. A fine musician, perhaps an accomplished violinist, should be best fitted, by virtue of his musical accomplishments, to evaluate the achievements of others in this area.

This, however, is not the case. Thorough knowledge of the subject area certainly is one requisite for valid measurement in that area, but in itself is not enough. The techniques of measurement also must be given attention if the mesaurements or evaluations are to be reliable and valid.

Because the techniques of measurement in academic music courses are essentially the same as those used in other areas in education, discussion in the present volume will be limited to a review of some general principles of classroom test construction, common methods of converting scores into grades, and suggestions for greater systematization of subjective evaluations important in music. Readers are urged to consult any of the references given for a more extensive coverage of testing and grading procedures.

Some Principles of Test Construction

The construction of a good test is a task which requires a great deal of careful planning. Good tests, whether objective or of the essay type, cannot be put together in a few moments. Generally, test items, once drafted, should be considered for a few days and revised as need becomes apparent. Some teachers find it helpful to add items to a tentative list as various segments of material are taken up in the progress of the course. In this way, test items are more likely to have a direct relevance to the material as it was presented than if the items must be fitted in retrospect. Further steps in good test construction follow.

Define objectives. The first step in the construction of a test is the definition of the expected outcomes or objectives of instruction for the period which the test is to cover. These objectives should be spelled out as explicitly as possible. Broad, general objectives must be broken down into more specific and concrete terms. While "understanding of music" may be a valid general goal for a course, it would be difficult to construct test items, of either objective or essay type, which could measure an outcome as broad as this. Before progress toward such a goal can be measured it is necessary to describe what is meant by "understanding of music"—what the recognizable characteristics of such understanding may be.

Balance the Test. The balance in test content should, in general, reflect the balance in instructional emphasis. After the objectives or outcomes of instruction have been defined, it is important to review the relative emphases given to these objectives.

A test should reflect these relative emphases. Those objectives which have received a major share of attention in instruction should take up a proportionate amount of the test content.

Consider the purpose of the test. Tests can serve different purposes. For example, a test may be written at one time for the purpose of grading students in a course. At another time, a test may be intended for diagnostic purposes, to reveal each student's weaknesses so that remedial steps can be taken. Conceivably, a test may attempt to serve both these purposes at once. Its purpose then is a dual one. Consideration of the purpose which the test is to serve, therefore, is important in planning its content. Items which are quite appropriate for grading purposes may not serve as satisfactorily if the intention is diagnosis, and still other modifications might be necessary if the test is to serve a dual purpose.

Consider the testing conditions. The wise teacher also will consider the conditions which will prevail at the time and in the place of testing. The physical facilities, such as the seating arrangement in the room, may influence the nature of the test content or the format of the measure. If room conditions tend to facilitate copying, for example, it may be advisable to use question forms which will minimize the possibilities of such cheating. Sometimes even a slight change in the arrangement of items may help to forestall copying.

A rather obvious consideration in planning tests in music courses is that of equipment available at the time of testing. If questions requiring any kind of aural discrimination or comprehension are to be included, the availability and satisfactory functioning of necessary equipment are of utmost importance. More than one music teacher has prepared material using, perhaps, his own phonograph and records, only to discover that in the classroom or test situation certain elements in the music are much less distinct, due to inadequacy of records and/or machine. It is advisable, therefore, to plan test items according to the equipment which will be available for use at the time of testing.

Among other conditions to be considered, of course, is the amount of time available for the test. The length of a test should be reasonable for the amount of time allotted for testing. Hurried answers, caused by excessive length of a test, frequently bring unreliable results.

Provide a range of difficulty. An informal classroom test or examination should present a range of difficulty appropriate for the group to which it is to be administered. Some items should be easy enough that they can be answered correctly by all students in the class; a few should measure the optimum achievement to be expected in the work covered. Some teachers believe that in order to measure optimum achievement a test should include items which cannot be answered by the best students. The rationale behind this belief is that if any student attains a perfect score, that student's power or knowledge probably has not been fully measured. Ideally, the general difficulty level of a test should be such that the average student attains about 50 per cent of the possible total score after allowing for chance. It is apparent that a test which presents a range of difficulty appropriate for one class may be either too easy or too difficult in general for another.

Arrange test items according to difficulty. A random order of items in a test is inadvisable. Whether the test is objective or of the essay type, the early questions or items should be the easier ones. Some testing authorities advise a gradational arrangement, from easiest item to most difficult. Such precision may be rather impracticable in arranging informal classroom tests, but every attempt should be made to begin with easy items and to reserve the most difficult for the late stages of the examination.

The basis for this principle is the psychological effect upon those taking the test. Relatively easy items at the beginning of a test tend to boost the morale of the students, while to be confronted at the outset with questions of greater difficulty may well be discouraging, especially to average and below average students. If the most difficult items are placed near the end of the test the poorer students already will have covered those questions within their levels of achievement before they encounter the difficult ones, if they reach them at all. Any resultant drop in morale thus will have a less serious effect upon the reliability of results. Since the purpose of the more difficult items is to discriminate among the better students, the failure of poorer students to reach such items will not jeopardize the validity of the test.

Check the wording of questions. The importance of clear wording of questions seems obvious, yet many informal tests are marked by deficiencies in this respect. The meaning of a question may seem quite explicit to its author who, after all, knows the answer, yet it may be ambiguous or obscure to the student who must make out that meaning before he can know in which direction to look for his answer. The test author, in checking the wording of his questions, must try to put himself in the place of the student, who has no foreknowledge of the questions other than his knowledge of the course material.

Care also must be taken, in writing a test item or question, that the wording does not provide unintended clues to the correct answer either of that item or of another. Sometimes the tense of a verb or the number of a noun, or some such clue in the form of the question itself may help the student to make a good guess. This danger, perhaps, more usually is present in writing objective tests, but the author of essay questions also must guard against it.

A danger which can ensnare the author of an essay type question is a wording which is too general to indicate the type or avenue of response desired. Although some teachers prefer essay type questions to objective forms because the former do permit greater freedom of response, it may be embarrassing to discover that some students have written an answer which is appropriate to the question yet which does not provide the information desired. Unless the test is limited to one or two questions covering a very limited segment of course material, it is best to direct the student's attention to a fairly specific line of response. Questions such as "Discuss the sonata-allegro form," or "Discuss opera in the Baroque Era," probably are too general for the usual type of course examination situation. Delimitations, such as "Describe the common key relationships of the sonata-allegro form," or "Describe the abuses which led to the reform of Baroque opera," are likely to provide more satisfactory results.

Consider scoring or grading problems. It is wise, in planning and writing a test, to consider what methods of scoring or grading will be used and under what circumstances that scoring or grading will be done. If any of the scoring will be done by assistants, for example, an objective type test is indicated, and the wording of items must be so explicit as to eliminate the necessity for any kind of interpretation of responses by the scorer. Scoring of objective tests generally is far simpler than that of essay type questions. In some instances, however, a slight modification in arrangement of individual items can significantly facilitate scoring. A multiple choice question, for example, can be presented in slightly different forms. In one case the student may be instructed to underline or encircle his answer. In the other, choices are provided with identifying letters or numbers, and the student is instructed to write the symbol associated with his choice of answer in a space provided at the left of the question. The example below shows a question arranged in these two ways:

In the sentence below underline the option which correctly completes the statement.

Opera originated at about the beginning of the (fifteenth; seventeenth; eighteenth) century.

By slightly rearranging the form of the answer of such questions, scoring can be speeded up.

In the space provided at the left of the sentence below, place the letter corresponding to the term which, in your opinion, correctly completes the statement.

b Opera originated at about the beginning of the (a) fifteenth; (b) seventeenth; (c) eighteenth century.

If the time available for scoring is short, the second arrangement can result in a significant saving, especially if the test is fairly long or the number of answer papers large.

Essay type questions usually present more problems in scoring than do objective items. If such a question is concocted hurriedly and without careful consideration of all of the problems involved, including that of scoring, the reliability and validity of the measurement may be seriously compromised. Questions which are too general and which permit too great freedom of response are extremely difficult to score reliably. Delimitation of the scope of the question has been discussed and need not be repeated here, but failure to consider this principle in essay question construction has contributed to the ineffectiveness of many examinations.

Although not directly related to the planning and construction of tests, a suggestion or two concerning procedures of scoring essay questions may be in order. Reliability of scoring usually is increased if the reader first makes a list of all elements which he would expect to find in the best answer possible. Values then should be assigned to these elements according to their respective importance. Answers then can be evaluated according to their coverage of these elements, each receiving a score appropriate to the adequacy of the coverage. The points awarded for the several elements then are totaled to provide the score for the question.

When an examination includes several questions it is advisable to read one question at a time, scoring that question on all papers before proceeding to another. In this way the scorer can concentrate on one area of the examination material at a time and thus achieve greater consistency in his marking. Some experienced teachers recommend a preliminary reading for the purpose of separating the papers into "above average," "average," and "below average" categories. By proceeding through the categories, preferably from top to bottom, distortion of scoring standards resulting from the juxtaposition of papers of widely differing quality is reduced. This procedure would be followed for each question. This system is too time consuming, perhaps, to be practicable in some situations, but it has much merit when circumstances allow its use.

Converting Test Scores Into Grades

Again, an extended discussion of grading seems beyond the scope of this book. There will be included here, therefore, only a brief review of one or two common methods of converting test scores into grades.

The debate over the respective merits of relative and absolute standards for grading seems to have been endowed with renewed vigor in recent years. Advocates of absolute standards have found in the mounting criticism of American education support for their view that relative standards are sinking standards, although no body of evidence is yet available to indict any grading system as the principal offender. Advocates of relative standards, on the other hand, long have held that absolute standards often are unrealistic and unfair.

It is not within the purpose of this work to discuss the respective merits of these conflicting opinions. Strong arguments can be marshaled for the support of either view. It is likely that factors present in the teaching situation, such as the nature of the course material or the general complexion of the class, frequently may aid in the choice of method for that particular instance. It will serve the present purpose to provide information concerning methods of deriving grades from test scores.

The percentage system probably is the most common system of grading by absolute standards. In some cases test scores may then be expressed directly as grades, provided the scores represent percentages of a perfect score. More often, however, per cent scores still must be converted into far fewer levels, each of greater extent. A five level type of grading probably is the most common, with five letters used to represent the several levels. A, B, C, D, and E, or A, B, C, D, and F are common systems. When percentages must be converted into grades expressed in these terms the teacher, or perhaps the school administration, may decide upon the points of division between levels. Thus, 90-100 may be an A, 80-90 a B, 70-80 a C, 60-70 a D, and below 60 an F. The setting of the standards is at the discretion of the teacher or of the school administration.

Most grading systems using relative standards are based on the normal curve of probability, although opinions differ as to just how this curve should be applied. Some use a relatively rigid application, setting out specified percentages of the distribution of scores to be included in each letter grade. Thus 7 per cent of the students in a class may be awarded A's, 23 per cent B's, 40 per cent C's, 23 per cent D's, and 7 per cent F's. Different percentages may be allotted to each grade level, and a number of different systems have been used. Note that this system is not like the percentage system of grading previously described. In that case the percentages referred to were percentage scores, percentages of a theoretically perfect attainment. In a relative system based on the normal curve, the percentages are parts of the distribution. In the sample division given here, the 7 per cent receiving A's refers to 7 per cent of the students taking the test, or of the students to be graded.

This rather rigid manner of applying the normal curve in grading fails to take into account differences in central tendency and variability among classes. For this reason many teachers prefer to use a curve which is computed, using the mean and either the standard deviation or the mean deviation. Such a curve is more flexible, adjusting to the shape of the distribution of the class to which it is applied.

The methods of computing standard deviations and mean deviations will not be given here. The reader will find these methods outlined in Chapter 3.

Once the standard deviation of a particular distribution has been computed it is applied for assigning grades on a five level basis as follows: all those scores falling within one unit of standard deviation about the mean ($\frac{1}{2}\sigma$ above, $\frac{1}{2}\sigma$ below M) receive C; those lying between $\frac{1}{2}\sigma$ above the mean to $1\frac{1}{2}\sigma$ above receive B; scores more than $1\frac{1}{2}\sigma$ above the mean receive A; from $\frac{1}{2}\sigma$ below the mean to $1\frac{1}{2}\sigma$ below receive D; and all scores more than $1\frac{1}{2}$ units of σ below the mean receive F.

A simple example will make this more clear. Suppose that on a test the mean of the scores attained is found to be 75, and the standard deviation of the group is 14. Letter grade equivalencies of scores then would be as follows:

97 - --- $=$ A	M $+$ $\frac{1}{2}\sigma = 82$
83 - 96 $=$ B	M $-$ $\frac{1}{2}\sigma = 68$
68 - 82 $=$ C	M $+$ $1\frac{1}{2}\sigma = 96$
54 - 67 $=$ D	M $-$ $1\frac{1}{2}\sigma = 54$
--- - 53 $=$ F	

The mean deviation is used in a similar manner. When the MD is used, grades can be assigned as follows:

A $=$ 2 MD and more above the mean
B $=$ $\frac{2}{3}$ MD above the mean to 2 MD above
C $=$ $\frac{2}{3}$ MD below the mean to $\frac{2}{3}$ MD above the mean
D $=$ $\frac{2}{3}$ MD below the mean to 2 MD below the mean
F $=$ 2 MD and more below the mean.

Thus, if a set of scores has a mean of 65 and a mean deviation of 9, grades will fall as follows:

A = 84 and above	M + ⅔ MD = 71
B = 72 - 83	M - ⅔ MD = 59
C = 59 - 71	M + 2 MD = 83
D = 47 - 58	M - 2 MD = 47
F = --- - 46	

When scores are converted into grades by means of a computed curve, it may be that the percentages of scores (i.e., number of scores) falling into the different grade levels may not be equal. That is to say, there may be, for example, more B's than D's. This is due to the fact that a computed curve adjusts to deviations from the normal distribution, i.e., to skewness of a distribution. This is an advantage in the use of a computed curve rather than an arbitrary curve.

The use of a curve in grading does not indicate the inevitable failure of a percentage of a particular group. The curve merely serves as a basis for sorting the scores into five categories. Whether or not any of these categories receives failing grades is a matter for the teacher to decide. Differences among classes, as well as those within classes, must be considered in grading, and suitable provision must be made for nontypical groups.

Applied music study presents the music teacher with some of his most formidable difficulties in grading. While few students at the elementary and secondary levels receive grades in applied music as such, improvement in performance ability is considered by many teachers to be an important part of more inclusive studies in music and, therefore, should carry significant weight when grades are assigned for these studies. How much weight should be given to performing ability in any more inclusive study is a matter of educational philosophy, and, as such, it is not directly pertinent to the present discussion. The problem of evaluating such improvement in performing ability, however, is much the same as that encountered by those high school and college instructors who must grade students directly in applied music.

In many situations, performance examinations play an important role in the determination of grades in this area of music study. Since such examinations are, in effect, auditions, discussion of grading in applied music will be deferred until the next chapter.

Grading in group performance courses, such as band, orchestra, or choir, is an especially vexing problem for many teachers. A two level grade system, e.g., satisfactory–unsatisfactory, is difficult enough to administer fairly and effectively, but a five level system seems to present insurmountable problems. Many teachers base such grades largely upon attendance and similar criteria. This approach, however, is highly questionable in that it fails to measure or evaluate progress toward the principal objectives of the course or activity. In addition measurement or evaluation of such progress seems virtually impossible in the circumstances which prevail in most group performance courses. In view of the nature of this type of course, a four or five level grading system seems impracticable. If grading is necessary in band, orchestra, or chorus, etc., a two level system is to be recommended. Even so, the grading must of necessity be largely subjective.

Summary

The necessity for grading in music courses, for diagnosis of student weaknesses, and for evaluation of teaching effectiveness makes valid techniques of measurement and evaluation as important to the music teacher as to teachers in other fields. General principles of test construction for music courses are similar to those which pertain in other subject areas. Probably most important among these is clear delineation of objectives to be attained, since measurement of progress obviously is impossible until the goal has been defined.

Methods of describing achievement in courses vary among different situations. Per cent scores and letter grades probably are among the most common. Test scores can be converted into letter grades by application of a curve, either with arbitrarily established distribution or with a distribution computed from the mean score.

Grading in group performance courses offers special problems. In view of the nature of such activities, no more than a two level distribution is to be recommended.

1. Outline the basic principles of test construction.

2. Select some area of course study in music and construct an objective type test for the measurement of achievement in this area.

3. Select another area and construct several essay type questions for the measurement of achievement in this area. Try these questions out on your classmates, and then discuss them in the light of the principles of test construction given in this chapter.

   N.B. Careful consideration should be given in questions 2 and 3 to selection of areas appropriate to the two types of questions to be written.

4. Arrange the following scores into a five level grade distribution.

50	83	62	79	90	84	46	63
73	67	53	81	77	61	74	54
65	72	92	49	83	59	80	79
80	43	50	57	64	72	89	83
77	88	75	62	53	85	72	66

   Use both an arbitrary curve and a computed curve, based on the SD.

5. Using a set of scores to be found among the questions and problems at the end of Chapter 3, work out a five level grade distribution based on the MD.

RECOMMENDED READINGS

Adams, G. S. and Torgerson, T. L. *Measurement and Evaluation.* New York: The Dryden Press, 1956. Chapter 12.

Lindquist, E. F. (ed.) *Educational Measurement.* Washington, D. C.: American Council on Education, 1951. Chapters 5-11, 13.

Stanley, Julian C. *Measurement in Today's Schools.* 4th ed. New York: Prentice-Hall, 1964. Chapters 6 and 8.

Thorndike, Robert L. and Hagen, Elizabeth. *Measurement and Evaluation in Psychology and Education.* 3rd ed. New York: John Wiley and Sons, Inc., 1969. Chapter 17.

CHAPTER 11

The Evaluation of Musical Performance

Many music teachers are called upon to evaluate musical performances of various kinds, either as a regular part of their teaching duties or upon specific occasions for specific purposes. In many college and university music departments, students in applied music are required to play periodically before a committee of faculty members who grade the performances. In a few high schools music teachers undertake the same kind of evaluative responsibility. Upon other occasions teachers conduct auditions for applicants for admission to an institution or for students seeking scholarships or other awards. Auditions frequently are used to select members for musical organizations or to place members within sections. Evaluation of musical performance, obviously, is an important function for many music teachers.

Techniques and procedures for evaluating performances vary, but in a great many cases it is to be feared that they are rather haphazard. The grading of applied music exams frequently is accomplished by informal discussion based upon general impressions of the performance, with little or no attempt at systematic evaluation. Although auditions for scholarships and other awards more often are rated by somewhat more methodical procedures, here, too, general impressions too frequently constitute the evaluative technique.

This does not imply that such examinations and auditions are carelessly conducted or regarded lightly. The conscientiousness and integrity of the examiners or auditioners, of course, will determine the care which is taken in evaluation. Evaluation through general impression is likely to be highly unreliable, however, even when performed by the most careful person of unimpeachable musical qualifications.

Problems

Musical performance, because of its very nature, is extremely difficult to evaluate reliably. Not only is it a highly complex affair, but certain aspects of it have so far defied precise definition, to say nothing of precise measurement. Although Seashore[1] expressed the hope some years ago that ways would be found to evaluate musical performances through objective measurement, no such techniques have been devised as yet, and it seems unlikely that they will be. Certain aspects of performance, such as accuracy, can be rated with some degree of objectivity. Other aspects, such as that intangible which is called "musicianship" by some and given various names by others, that something which lies beyond accuracy and which distinguishes the truly musical performance from the merely accurate, remain beyond the scope of objective measurement.

Further complicating the reliable evaluation of musical performance is the lack of definite standards of quality for various elements of performance. Differences of opinion exist as to what is, for example, the best quality of tone for a given medium. Although such differences usually fall within relatively narrow limits, they are prevalent even among highly qualified observers. Thus, even though it is possible to analyze a tone and to identify its constituent parts, i.e., its overtones in their relative strengths,

---

[1]Carl E. Seashore. *Psychology of Music.* New York: McGraw-Hill Book Co., 1939, pp. 9-10.

objective evaluation of it still is impossible because of lack of definite, generally agreed upon, standards of excellence.

Evaluation of musical performances, therefore, must remain largely subjective in nature. Improvement must come through the replacement of general impressions by ratings arrived at by use of more systematic procedures. These ratings, in the final analysis, still will be subjective, but the use of more methodical techniques by well-qualified auditioners should result in more accurate and more reliable decisions.

Rating Scales

The best tool for evaluating musical performances seems to be a kind of rating scale which will help auditors to systematize their judgments and also aid in ensuring that all auditors evaluate a performance on the same basis, i.e., give attention to the same elements of performance and weight the elements in the same way. Two types of scale are used. On one type the auditor indicates on a graduated scale the quality level of each relevant element of performance. On the other, the same purpose is served by awarding a number of points for each aspect of performance to be weighed in the evaluation.

In either case, the first step in constructing such a rating scale is the identification of the elements of performance to be rated. An instrumental solo performance thus might be rated on tone, intonation, technique, and interpretation. Since each of these elements is in some degree a complex, further analysis into subdivisions might be in order for some. Technique and interpretation, for example, probably are too general and should be broken down into some of their constituents. Since beauty and control of tone are not always directly related, some teachers might prefer to evaluate tone separately for each of these aspects rather than to take a more general approach. Just how many elements of performance should be rated is, to some extent, a matter of opinion. The purpose of the rating sometimes will aid in determining the number to be used.

One important consideration in determining the number of elements to be rated is that all of these elements will be present throughout a performance and all will, in effect, be rated simultaneously. That is to say, the auditor will not rate tone during one segment of a performance, technique during another, interpretation during a third segment, etc. Certain elements may gain a greater share of the auditor's attention at various times, but ratings of the quality of each element generally will be made throughout the performance. It is well, therefore, to keep the number of elements to be rated fairly small. Excessive subdivision increases the complexity of the rating procedure by causing the listener's attention to be directed simultaneously toward too many specifics. The number and kinds of elements to be rated also should be appropriate to the purpose of the audition. An audition for entrance to a school, for example, probably will not emphasize the same elements as would one for admission to, or placement in, a musical organization.

Opinions will differ, too, as to the relative importance of the rated elements of performance. Some auditors will give greater weight to tone, others to technique or interpretation or some other element. When more than one auditor is to rate a performance there must be prior agreement, of course, as to the elements to be rated and the respective weights which these elements are to carry in the final evaluation. Once again, the purpose which the audition is to serve often will have some influence upon the weighting of the elements to be rated.

A suggested rating scale for wind instrument performance is presented in Figure 9. The list of elements to be rated would be somewhat different, of course, for other media of performance. Some auditors, too, might prefer to rate elements other than those suggested here. Since standardized forms for this purpose are not in wide use, those made up for specific situations or occasions may conform to the wishes of those who are to use them.

Letter ratings from A to E may be used instead of numbers. If this procedure is followed, however, letters must be converted into numerical values for averaging in order to arrive at a final rating. The use of letters, therefore, imposes an additional step. If auditors feel, however, that they could rate more comfortably on a letter scale, there should be no serious objection.

Name.. Instrument......................

Rate each of the elements of performance listed below using a five point scale. Place in the space provided beside each element of performance a number from one to five, indicating your estimate of the quality of that element in this performance. One (1) indicates the lowest level, five (5) the highest level of performance. *Use whole numbers only.*

Tone............................

Intonation............................

Technique

      Tonguing............................

      Finger or slide dexterity............................

Interpretation

      Phrasing............................

      Sensitivity to line............................

      Dynamic nuance............................

Average rating............................ (The sum of the separate ratings divided by seven)

Figure 9. Suggested Rating Scale for Wind Instruments.

This scale might be set up in a slightly different form without significantly altering its function. Figure 10 illustrates such a modification.

Name.. Instrument.........................

Place a check mark on the line beside each listed element of performance at the number which indicates your rating of this element in this performance. *Please check only at numbered points, not at intermediate points.* 1 indicates the lowest level of performance quality, 5 the highest level.

Tone |..............|..............|..............|..............|
             1.   2.   3.   4.   5.

Intonation |..............|..............|..............|..............|
             1.   2.   3.   4.   5.

Technique

    Tonguing |..............|..............|..............|..............|
             1.   2.   3.   4.   5.

    Finger or
    slide dexterity |..............|..............|..............|..............|
             1.   2.   3.   4.   5.

Interpretation

    Phrasing |..............|..............|..............|..............|
             1.   2.   3.   4.   5.

    Sensitivity to line |..............|..............|..............|..............|
             1.   2.   3.   4.   5.

    Dynamic nuance |..............|..............|..............|..............|
             1.   2.   3.   4.   5.

Average rating........................... (Add separate ratings and divide the sum by seven)

Figure 10. Suggested Rating Scale for Wind Instrument Performance.

Formulators of some rating scales permit or encourage the indication of intermediate values instead of asking raters to check only at numbered places, as suggested in the scale illustrated in Figure 10. This is, in effect, using a finer scale or a scale with more points. It calls for finer degrees of discrimination. The question inevitably arises: "How fine distinctions can be made reliably by subjective methods?"

It is possible to use a larger or a smaller number of ratings, or degrees of quality, in scales of these types. Some writers have expressed the belief that, for some purposes at least, three levels are sufficient for rating scales. For auditioning or adjudicating in music, five levels do not seem excessive. While a greater number might be used, this is likely to increase the unreliability of the ratings. Five, furthermore, is convenient for most grading systems.

The order of ratings sometimes is reversed. That is, *one* may be used for the highest level and *five* for the lowest. Since such scales, at least in music, are not in wide use at present, no really standardized form has been established. In developing a form for use in a particular situation, either order would seem to be satisfactory. The order, however, should be stated explicitly, and it must be clearly understood by those using the form. If letters are used instead of numbers, it probably is better to use A for the highest level and E for the lowest. This is a very common concept, used in many applications. To conform to this widespread practice, therefore, probably is less confusing to most auditors.

Still another form, in which points are awarded for each element, sometimes is used. There seems, however, to be no advantage to such a system for two or three reasons. Unless larger numbers are used, there really is no difference between this form and the one given in Figure 9. If larger numbers are used, there is the implication of finer degrees of discrimination. Sometimes points as great in number as one hundred are used for each element. Not only does this imply finer degrees of discrimination than actually can be made, but it is unrealistic. In such cases, ratings usually are made by multiples of five or ten, and very often the lowest fifty or sixty points are not used at all. Thus, the ratings probably are less valid than those made on a five point scale.

Rating scales used in other fields frequently use verbal descriptions for the various levels instead of a simple numerical or letter scale. In the present application this method might take a form such as the following.

Consistently out of tune	Many serious deviations in pitch	Several serious deviations in pitch	A few deviations	Very few or no deviations

Intonation |..................|..................|..................|..................|

There is considerable doubt, however, that such verbalizations are more meaningful with reference to musical performance than a simple five point scale. Different levels of some aspects of musical performance, such as tone or interpretation, would be even more difficult to describe verbally than is intonation. While verbalizations are preferred by testing specialists in other areas, therefore, it seems likely that the simple five place scale serves as well as any method for rating musical performance.

When a performance is rated by several auditors, as in an applied music examination, it is preferable that each auditor work independently, using a separate rating sheet. The independent ratings then should be averaged to produce a single final rating. If any discussion of an examinee is necessitated, perhaps to explain unusual circumstances, this should take place before the performance so that the individual ratings can be made accordingly. In any case such an attempt to weigh extraneous factors in the evaluation of a performance is to be questioned. Such attempts inevitably lower the reliability and the validity of the ratings. Reliability of ratings can be increased by increasing the number of auditors, assuming, of course, that all will be well qualified. The addition of auditors of questionable qualifications obviously lowers both the reliability and the validity of the ratings.

Scoring of scales of this type is a simple process. It can be carried out either by the auditor or by someone else to whom this responsibility is assigned. The score, or final rating, would consist simply of the mean of the ratings for the several elements listed. Thus, if ratings of 3, 3, 2, 2, 4, 4, and 2 had been awarded the respective elements of a performance, using the rating scale given in Figure 9, the final rating for this performance would be the mean of these several ratings. For this performance the final rating would be 2.86 or, rounded off, 3.

If it has been decided that certain elements of the performance are to be given greater weight, then the mean will be weighted accordingly. The simplest method of weighting a rating or score in the final or average rating is to count the weighted score a number of times corresponding to the weight which that element is to carry. Thus, if it had been decided to give Tone three times as much importance as each of the other elements in the foregoing example, the rating of 3 for Tone would be added in three times in totaling the scores. Since this, in effect, increases the number of scores or ratings contributing to the mean, this must be taken into account in dividing the sum. In the example, then, the weighted sum of the individual ratings, 26, would be divided by 9. The weighted mean then would be 2.77.

In rounding off 2.77 to the nearest integral number, the final rating still would be 3. The effect of the weighting in this example, therefore, is negligible. This is likely to be true in most cases, although it depends mainly on the extent of the weighting and the number of separate elements rated. There is considerable doubt, therefore, that weighting of elements is worthwhile in using a rating scale of this type.

It must be kept in mind that rating scales such as those suggested here by no means represent objective measurement of musical performance. They can, at best, serve as guides to better subjective evaluation. Even with such guides, subjective evaluations will continue to be rather unreliable, but some such sort of analysis in rating seems far preferable to the general impressions which too frequently serve as the basis for evaluation.

Course Grades in Applied Music

A somewhat different problem is encountered by the teacher who must grade students in applied music courses. The problem in this case is that of evaluating progress or achievement in performing ability over a period of time.

Development of systematic procedures which will result in reliable evaluations of such achievement presents extreme difficulty.

Some applied music teachers record a grade for each lesson and then average out these grades to arrive at a final grade. This method represents an effort, at least, toward some sort of systematization in grading.

There are several objections to this method, however. Progress in musical performance is not always gradual or even over a period of time. Students frequently seem to make little or no progress for several weeks, only to make a sudden leap forward. This is particularly true in the development of various aspects of technique. While it sometimes is caused, of course, by unevenness of effort, it is as often due to the nature of this type of learning. An average of weekly grades frequently will fail to take sufficient account of such unevenness in progress and in this way, perhaps, will result in a final grade which is lower than the student really deserves.

On the other hand, a general estimate of what the student has accomplished in the course of a semester or in any other period seems an extremely unreliable "method" of assigning grades. Such an estimate inevitably is influenced by the instructor's thoughts or feelings of the moment. Furthermore, even with the most careful thinking it is extremely difficult, to say the least, to remember and evaluate over a period of this length.

Unfortunately, at present there seems to be no real solution to this dilemma. Certainly, the recording of grades for shorter periods for use in determining final grades is to be recommended. It seems equally important, however, that in "averaging" the final grade from these periodic ratings, recognition be made of unevenness in progress. The periodic ratings should serve as a guide, rather than as a rigid system.

SUMMARY

Many music teachers frequently are called upon to evaluate musical performances. Applied music examinations and auditions held for various purposes are among the most common occasions for such evaluations.

Evaluation of performance is of necessity largely subjective. Too frequently, applied music exams and auditions are rated rather haphazardly through general impressions. More systematic procedures are needed in order to produce more reliable evaluations. This is true, also, of course grading in applied music.

QUESTIONS AND PROBLEMS FOR DISCUSSION AND PRACTICE

1. Make out a rating scale to be used for rating performance in each of the following media: wind instrument; string instrument; drum; piano; voice.
2. From your own experience as student and teacher, critically review common methods of grading applied music. Include both the grading of examinations and the assigning of course grades.
3. Suggest some procedures which would improve grading in applied music.

RECOMMENDED READINGS

Cronbach, Lee J. *Essentials of Psychological Testing*. Third edition. New York: Harper and Bros., 1970. Chapter 17.

Travers, Robert M. W. *Educational Measurement*. New York: Macmillan, 1955. pp. 215-222.

CHAPTER 12

Conclusion

Although the nature of music and musical performance may seem to make inappropriate attempts to measure or evaluate in any precise way its various aspects, measurement and evaluation are essential tools in music education. Measurement of aptitude for purposes of prediction makes possible greatly improved guidance, and measurement and evaluation of achievement are essential for appraisal both of student achievement and of teaching effectiveness. The development of reliable and valid techniques for measurement and evaluation of aptitude and achievement in music has been, and continues to be, an important concern of music educators and psychologists alike. Understanding of principles of measurement and of important concepts in measurement and evaluation in music are essential to the music teacher or supervisor for the intelligent use of existing measures as well as for the evaluation of those which may appear in years to come. They are essential to the teacher, too, for the improvement of his own techniques of evaluating student achievement in regular music study.

It is important that those who might have need of objective measures of musical aptitude and of musical achievement understand the significant differences among tests as well as the limitations of the various measures and batteries. With the appearance of additional tests of aptitude or talent put forth by instrument manufacturers and distributors, a bewildering array of such measures now is available to the music teacher. It is unfortunate that some teachers, lacking the knowledge essential for intelligent analysis and evaluation of these tests, frequently turn to measures of unsound basis and, consequently, of little value. Ability to distinguish between tests based on sound psychological principles and constructed by means of careful scientific procedures, and those resulting from the unsubstantiated beliefs and extemporized procedures of individuals, will enable the teacher to avoid the waste of time and the misleading implications frequently resulting from the use of this latter type of measure.

It is important, too, that the teacher understand what can reasonably be expected from any test. Failing this, inaccurate interpretation of results leading to erroneous assumptions may mislead the teacher into unsound guidance practices. The measurement of aptitude for musical accomplishment, especially, is an extremely difficult task. The varieties of accomplishment with their different demands, the complexity of musical performance, and the lack of objective standards all complicate the task of the aptitude test author. Teachers must be careful that, in their desire to obtain as much information as possible in a short time, they do not become overanxious for the quick, easy answer. Such an attitude could lead to acceptance of tests which purport to measure much but which, in attempting to measure more than can be measured by one test, actually measure nothing with a satisfactory degree of accuracy.

Understanding of tests and testing principles, and especially of the limitations of current measures, will help the teacher to avoid certain questionable practices too often associated with test administration by commercially minded advisors. The use of aptitude measures, or of the results of aptitude measures, as a means of "selling" the instrumental program or any other program, might well come under the heading of unethical practices in music education. This is true even when the measures used are based upon sound psychological theories and follow scientific principles of test construction. When the measures themselves are of a highly questionable nature, the gravity of the offense is quite obvious. Publicizing of test scores inevitably leads to misinterpretation on the part of a general public unfamiliar with testing principles and with statistical analysis and interpretation of test results. Test scores should be confided only to those persons immediately concerned, and then only in private conference or by some other means through which clear understanding can be assured. Tests are for the teacher, to enable him to know better, and thus to guide better, his students. Encouragement of persons shown by valid tests to possess significant aptitude is a legitimate procedure in guidance. Even then, however, such encouragement should be qualified by consideration of all factors involved. Discouragement of seemingly low aptitudes should be approached with a similar view. Quite obviously, thorough understanding of any measuring devices used, of what they actually measure and how well, as well as adequate knowledge of the field of endeavor involved is an essential prerequisite to this type of guidance.

It is to be hoped that continued research in this field will lead to the development of measures which will yield more comprehensive information from testings of practical length. Recent trends indicate that future attempts will continue to place greater emphasis upon actual musical functions rather than upon simple analysis of sensory abilities. In view of the important contribution which valid measures of musical aptitude can make to the field of music education, it is to be hoped that music teachers will lend encouragement to attempts to develop more satisfactory measures.

Continued research is needed, also, to effect improvements in classroom tests and in the evaluation of musical performance. In the latter area especially, present methods are often too haphazard. Evaluation of musical performance probably never can be entirely objective due to its very nature, but systematic procedures can improve the reliability, and thus the validity, of such appraisals. It is to be hoped that clear definition of standards and further research into procedures will help to effect still greater improvement.

It is inevitable, however, that no matter how great the improvement in measures, whether standardized or teacher made, their value always will depend upon the manner in which they are used.

An intelligent approach to the use of tests can be summed up in the following principles:

1. Definition of objectives always is an essential preliminary to measurement. The ends for which the measuring process is to be used must be clearly defined before tools for the task can be selected or constructed.

2. Results of tests should be regarded as tentative. The measuring devices currently available are imprecise in varying degrees, and those of the future undoubtedly will be also. Measures must be used with this in mind, and results must be interpreted accordingly.

3. Tests are limited in the information which they can provide. It is important, therefore, that the user be aware of the limitations of any test which he uses and that he interpret the results in the light of this knowledge. Tests must be viewed as but one source of information for guidance. Tests must be supplemented by other means such as informal observations, personality and interest inventories, and ratings in order to gain as complete knowledge as possible of the individuals to be advised.

4. The need for interpretation of results of measurement must never be overlooked. Tests and other measuring procedures are tools, and perception and insight are necessary for the intelligent use of such tools. The more complex the purposes for which the measures are to be used, the greater the number of tools needed and the greater the skill required for their intelligent application.

Index

Ability to sing melody
  in measurement of musical aptitude, 105
Absolute pitch
  in measurement of musical aptitude, 105
Administration of a test
  ease of, as criterion of evaluation, 73
Aesthetic sensitivity
  in measurement of musical aptitude, 104-105
Aliferis, James, 174
Aliferis Music Achievement Test—College Entrance Level, 162-164, 174
  description, 162-163
  manual, 163
  norms, 163
  reliability, 163
  scoring, 163
Aliferis-Stecklein Music Achievement Test—College Midpoint Level, 164-165, 174

description, 164-165
manual, 165
reliability, 165
Allen, Richard D., 153, 175
Applied music courses, grades in, 197-198
Applied music exams, 189-190
Attenuation, correction for, 27
Auditions, 189
Average deviation, 24

Beach Music Test, 149-151, 174
  description, 149-151
  norms, 151
  reliability, 151
  validity, 151
Bentley, Arnold, 139, 146
Bentley, R. R.
  and Farnum Music Notation Test, 171
  and Kwalwasser Music Talent Test, 131
  and Musical Aptitude Test by Whistler and Thorpe, 130